REVIVING THE DEATH PENALTY

Gary E. McCuen

IDEAS IN CONFLICT SERIES

publications inc.
411 Mallalieu Drive
Hudson, Wisconsin 54016

Illustration & photo credits

Amnesty International 107, 120, 127, Carol & Simpson 13, 75, 130, Daily World 86, Foremost Art 79, Fortune News 34, 69, 93, The Guardian 23, 28, Los Angeles Times Syndicate 9, Massachusetts Labor Committee 48, Mennonite Central Committee of the U.S. & Canada 63, Minneapolis Star & Tribune 44, St. Louis Post Dispatch 39

© 1985 by Gary E. McCuen Publications, Inc.
411 Mallalieu Drive • Hudson, Wisconsin 54016 •
(715) 386-5662
International Standard Book Number 0-86596-052-6
Printed in the United States of America

CONTENTS

CHAPTER 4 CAPITAL PUNISHMENT IN FOREIGN COUNTRIES

REASONING SKILL DEVELOPMENT

*These activities may be used as individualized study guides
for students in libraries and resource centers or as discussion
catalysts in small group and classroom discussions.*

IDEAS in ⊕NFLICT ®

This series features ideas in conflict on political, social and moral issues. It presents counterpoints, debates, opinions, commentary and analysis for use in libraries and classrooms. Each title in the series uses one or more of the following basic elements:

Introductions that present an issue overview giving historic background and/or a description of the controversy.

Counterpoints and debates carefully chosen from publications, books, and position papers on the political right and left to help librarians and teachers respond to requests that treatment of public issues be fair and balanced.

Symposiums and forums that go beyond debates that can polarize and oversimplify. These present commentary from across the political spectrum that reflect how complex issues attract many shades of opinion.

A global emphasis with foreign perspectives and surveys on various moral questions and political issues that will help readers to place subject matter in a less culture-bound and ethno-centric frame of reference. In an ever shrinking and interdependent world, understanding and cooperation are essential. Many issues are global in nature and can be effectively dealt with only by common efforts and international understanding.

Reasoning skill study guides and discussion activities provide ready made tools for helping with critical reading and evaluation of content. The guides and activities deal with one or more of the following:

RECOGNIZING AUTHOR'S POINT OF VIEW

INTERPRETING EDITORIAL CARTOONS

VALUES IN CONFLICT

WHAT IS EDITORIAL BIAS?

WHAT IS SEX BIAS?

WHAT IS POLITICAL BIAS?

WHAT IS ETHNOCENTRIC BIAS?

WHAT IS RACE BIAS?

WHAT IS RELIGIOUS BIAS?

From across **the political spectrum** varied sources are presented for research projects and classroom discussions. Diverse opinions in the series come from magazines, newspapers, syndicated columnists, books, political speeches, foreign nations, and position papers by corporations and non-profit institutions.

About The Editor

Gary E. McCuen is an editor and publisher of anthologies for public libraries and curriculum materials for schools. Over the past 14 years his publications of over 200 titles have specialized in social, moral and political conflict. They include books, pamphlets, cassettes, tabloids, filmstrips and simulation games, many of them designed from his curriculums during 11 years of teaching junior and senior high school social studies. At present he is the editor and publisher of the *Ideas in Conflict* series and the *Editorial Forum* series.

A HISTORY OF CAPITAL PUNISHMENT

by Franklin E. Zimring and Michael Laurence

Historical Context

Use of the death penalty has declined throughout the industrial Western world since the 19th century, and nearly every European nation has either formally abolished the death penalty for civil crimes or has abandoned it in practice.

Despite the current American revival of capital punishment, the United States has contributed to the trend toward abolition. Indeed, when Michigan joined the Union in 1847, it had already earned the distinction of being the first abolitionist jurisdiction in the Western world. The United States experience in the 20th century also parallels the long-term, worldwide decline in executions. Since the peak years of 1935 and 1936, when states conducted 199 executions, the number of yearly executions in this country decreased continuously, culminating in a de facto moratorium between 1967 and 1977. Abandonment of capital punishment appeared complete with the United States Supreme Court's decision in *Furman v. Georgia* in 1972. In *Furman,* the Court invalidated state death penalty statutes, as then administered, because death sentences were "freakishly" and arbitrarily imposed. The eighth amendment of the Constitution prohibits a criminal justice system that imposes death sentences with the same consistency as the likelihood of being "struck by lightning."

Reprinted from a National Institute of Justice CRIME FILE Study Guide on the Death Penalty, by Franklin E. Zimring and Michael Laurence, University of California at Berkeley.

THE OTHER DEATH PENALTY

Don Hesse, © 1976, *St. Louis Globe Democrat.* Reprinted with permission, Los Angeles Times Syndicate.

Contrary to the expectations of many observers, *Furman* did not resolve the death penalty controversy. In *Gregg v. Georgia,* decided four years after *Furman,* the Supreme Court revived capital punishment. The *Gregg* Court held that various state capital punishment laws enacted in response to *Furman* sufficiently reduced the randomness permitted by the previous statutes. The Court concluded that the "new" death penalty statutes complied with Constitutional requirements, and thus it permitted states to resume executions. The state statutes approved by the Court differ from prior penal codes in permitting imposition of capital punishment only for murder, stating grounds to be considered by a trier-of-fact in making the death penalty decision, and specifying reasonably specific criteria that must be shown to apply if capital punishment is to be imposed.

The Current Situation

The United States is now in a transition between enacting the death penalty in the abstract and actually administering the punishment in a manner consistent with society's morals and with constitutional requirements. In the decade following *Gregg*, some states slowly began to implement a policy dormant for the previous 10 years and, with the Supreme Court's approval, hesitantly resumed executions. Indeed, the first prisoner executed in the post-*Gregg* era, Gary Gilmore, demanded that the Utah authorities execute him in 1977. Momentum, though negligible at first, eventually provided the impetus for resuming executions. There were no executions in 1978, followed by two in 1979, none in 1980, one in 1981, and two in 1982. The rate more than doubled in 1983 to five. Then in 1984, partially due to the Supreme Court's efforts to accelerate the appeals process and diminish federal oversight, the number of executions increased to 21. The 1984 rate does not appear to be atypical of the future; by mid-year, states had executed 13 prisoners in 1985.

Just as the rate of executions presents an interesting pattern, so too does the distribution of states administering those sentences. Although 39 states currently authorize the death sentence, by mid-1985 only 12 have executed any prisoners. Moreover, of the 47 executions since 1976, 34 have been performed in four states, Florida (13), Texas (9), Louisiana (6), and Georgia (6). The concentration of executions in the South is also illustrated by the remaining executions; the South has conducted all of the last 43 executions, and the last execution outside of that region occurred in 1981. The South's domination of executions corresponds closely to the distribution of executions in the 1950s. The four states responsible for 72 percent of the post-*Gregg* executions were also among the top six executing states of the 1950s.

Though the South dominated execution statistics, its share of prisoners sentenced to death is somewhat more modest. Southern states accounted for 62 percent of the 1,540 prisoners under a death sentence as of August 1, 1985. Several other states maintain significant death row populations. For example, 173 prisoners have been sentenced to die in California's gas chamber, the third largest death row population in the country. Illinois and Pennsylvania, each with 77 prisoners on death row, are ranked sixth. Despite the large number of prisoners sentenced to death in these states, none have been executed.

Large death rows are apparently not closely connected to execution policy outside the South. Utah, one of the three non-Southern states to have carried out death penalties, has only five prisoners currently on death row. The other two non-Southern states that have executed, Indiana and Nevada, maintain relatively small death rows of 31 and 28 prisoners, respectively. Even in the South, a small death row population appears to be irrelevant to the state's execution policy. For example, Louisiana's six executions since 1976 rank it third among all states, but its death row population of 41 ranks 14th. By comparison, the neighboring state of Alabama has 72 prisoners awaiting execution—but has performed only two executions (1983 and 1984). Florida, by contrast, leads the nation in both executions (13) since 1976 and the number of prisoners sentenced to death (221).

America is poised at the crossroads in the death penalty controversy. In the long term, it appears to be following the Western world trend toward abolition. This conclusion can be demonstrated by the relatively low execution rates and long-term decline in the penalty's use. On the other hand, the high numbers on death row and the short-term increase in executions may signal a return to the execution rates of the 1950s, if not the 1930s.

The Capital Punishment Debate

There are four major issues in the capital punishment debate.

1. **Deterrence.** A major purpose of criminal punishment is to deter future criminal conduct. The deterrence theory assumes that a rational person will avoid criminal behavior if the *severity* of the punishment for that behavior and the perceived *certainty* of receiving the punishment combine to outweigh the benefits of the illegal conduct. Although the accuracy of the many assumptions behind the deterrence approach is itself a matter of dispute, the deterrent value of a particularly severe punishment, the death penalty, is important in the current controversy.

The deterrence achieved by using the death penalty must be examined in the context of the entire criminal justice system. For the death penalty to deter first-degree (or capital) murders, the killer must know of the penalty's application to the crime and must believe that the certainty of punishment is sufficient to create an unacceptable risk. Without such awareness, the killer will probably not be deterred. One further factor must be considered when assessing a penalty's deterrent impact. Any deterrent value must be judged in the context of alternatives; if a

11

lesser penalty achieves the same or a greater level of deterrence, no deterrent justification supports the enhanced punishment.

Possibly because deterrence is ingrained in our lives—for example, children are punished for violating the family rules—a majority of the public supports the death penalty because they consider it an effective deterrent. Supporters contend the death sentences and executions heighten the risk of punishment in a potential killer's mind. By threatening to take the killer's life, society "ups the ante" of killing another.

Studies of the deterrent effect of the death penalty have been conducted for several years, with varying results. As opponents of the death penalty argue, most of these studies have failed to produce evidence that the death penalty deters murders more effectively than the threat of protracted imprisonment. Various reasons might explain this conclusion. First, the weight assigned to the enhanced severity is only marginal since the comparable punishment is, in most cases, life imprisonment without possibility of parole, or very long sentences. Second, the other key element in the deterrence theory, the perceived certainty of imposing the sentence, is rather low for most murders for a number of reasons: many crimes remain unsolved; the defendant may escape apprehension; evidence may be lacking or inadmissible; plea bargaining may enable the defendant to avoid capital punishment; the jury may acquit or not impose the penalty; and appeals and clemency petitions may delay or preclude execution. The actual probability that a murderer will receive a death sentence is quite low and the risk of being executed even smaller, about 1 per 1,000 killings in 1984. Even when the certainty of punishment is higher, many killers might refuse to believe they will be apprehended, let alone executed. Third, the assumption of rationality on which deterrence theories are based may not be valid for many killers.

Supporters of the death penalty make two principal arguments about deterrence: that common sense alone suggests that people fear death more than other punishments and that, when studies fail to resolve the issue, executions should continue on the assumption that a small saving of innocent lives will result.

The deterrence issue, important as it is, will not be resolved by statistical studies. Both supporters and opponents agree that the deterrent value of the death penalty is unproved. Furthermore, the limits on studies of this type, as well as the complexity of the problem, will probably prevent any definitive "scientific" resolution of the deterrence issue in the future.

2. **Retribution**. The central justification of capital punishment is the need for society to express sufficient condemnation for heinous murders. Supporters of the death penalty contend that the only proper societal response to the most vile murders is the most severe sanction possible. Thus, society should literally interpret the "eye for an eye" principle when an individual takes a life, society's moral balance will remain upset until the killer's life is also taken.

Although death penalty opponents agree that some punishment, even a harsh one, should be imposed on offenders of society's norms, they disagree with the assumption that society can express its outrage with a vile crime only by inflicting a mortal punishment. Opponents further claim that society's goal of greater morality, rather than being advanced, is actually defeated when its expression of outrage for the taking of one life is the taking of another life. Indeed, opponents argue that the state's act is, in some respects, more calculated and cold-blooded than that of many murderers.

Though individuals must judge for themselves the proper role of retribution in criminal justice, the question is the same for everyone: At what point do we stop trying to match horrible criminal actions with horrible government actions? Taken to the extreme, a retribution theory might require the state to kill the offender in the exact same manner in which the victim was

13

killed. Of course, this position is morally unacceptable to most people; our sense of outrage may be sufficiently expressed by less horrible forms of punishment. The key issue is whether punishment short of killing offenders sufficiently expresses social condemnation of murder in modern America.

3. **Arbitrariness**. The major reason the Supreme Court invalidated the nation's death penalty laws in *Furman v. Georgia* was that death sentences were imposed in an arbitrary and capricious manner. Death penalty opponents claim that the "new" death penalty statutes have failed to reduce the randomness inherent in selecting who shall die. Armed with a decade of experience with the revised statutes, opponents point to continuing inconsistent application. For example, of the 1,540 death row inmates, 42 percent are black, though blacks constitute only 12 percent of the population at large. Moreover, those convicted of killing white victims are more than four times as likely to receive death sentences as are those convicted of killing blacks. An even greater apparent disparity exists between the genders of death row inmates: though women constitute 16 percent of those who commit murder, they make up only 1.3 percent of the death row population. (This disparity may be less stark than appears when the types of murders committed by men and by women are taken into account; murders by men are much more likely to involve predatory crime.)

Supporters of the penalty reply that murder is not evenly committed by both sexes and both races, and that over-representation in one death sentence group may simply mean that other killers are being improperly spared. Opponents respond that a punishment unjustly administered cannot foster the community's sense of retributive justice or notions of equality. Supporters of the penalty suggest these problems call for greater efforts toward evenhanded administration of the death penalty, not abolition of the penalty. Opponents deny that evenhanded execution is possible in any criminal justice system.

4. **Danger of mistake**. The death penalty's unique character is its finality and irrevocability. Unlike a prison term, which can be commuted at any time, the death penalty, once executed, cannot be recalled. Thus, the irrevocability of the punishment heightens the dangers involved with wrongful convictions.

Opponents of the death penalty argue that the possibility of executing an innocent person requires abolishing the penalty. They contend that the likelihood of executing someone who does not deserve to die—that is, one whose crime does not fall within the definition of capital murder—is quite high. And

14

though the person might be guilty of a serious crime, imposing the death penalty in this case is wrong. The less probable though more morally unacceptable scenario is that a state will execute someone who did not commit the crime. Opponents cite studies concluding that there have been more than 100 cases of an innocent person wrongly convicted of murder; in at least 31 of these, a death sentence was imposed. More important, it is claimed that at least eight innocent individuals have been executed. Opponents argue that the likelihood of executing even one innocent person warrants rejecting the penalty.

Supporters, for the most part, argue that the current administration of the death penalty contains adequate safeguards to protect against miscarriages of justice. They cite the numerous levels of review and the scrutiny given to each death sentence. In addition, some supporters claim that the slight possibility of executing an innocent person must be accepted as the price of maintaining a credible criminal justice system.

Minor Issues in the Capital Punishment Debate

Three other issues frequently encountered in the death penalty debate seem of lesser import. These are questions of comparative cost, whether capital punishment plays a crucial role in reducing crime by incapacitating offenders, and the impact of capital punishment on the rate of violent crime.

The debate about cost has curious origins. Some popular sentiment supports the death penalty on the impression that it is less costly to execute prisoners than to maintain them in prison for life terms. Abolitionists, by contrast, have sought to demonstrate that executions in the modern United States are more costly than long prison terms, chiefly because of the cost of special legal processing. The argument is unimportant because the small number of executions or life sentences involved is an insubstantial part of the criminal justice budget.

That the alternative to the death penalty is secure confinement for long periods, in many states for life without parole, makes it unlikely that capital punishment decreases crime through incapacitation. Whether or not executed, the offender's dangerousness will not be inflicted on the community.

Furthermore, the small number of candidates for execution under any conceivable regime of capital punishment means that executions cannot be regarded as a way of reducing the incidence of violent crimes in the United States. Violent crimes number in the millions, prison populations in the hundreds of thousands. Executions, even at their 20th century peak, were under 200 a year. The issue of the death penalty is thus largely a symbolic one in the crime control debate, but fundamentally important nonetheless.

CHAPTER 2

HUMANE EXECUTIONS AND MEDICAL ETHICS

OVERVIEW

METHODS OF EXECUTION: THE MEDICAL AND BIOLOGICAL EFFECTS

Harold Hillman

Harold Hillman is the reader in physiology at the University of Surrey in England and the editor-in-chief of the Resuscitation *medical journal. He describes the various techniques of execution and the probable biological and medical effects on the victims.*

Points to Consider

1. What methods of execution are now in use?
2. Is there a humane form of execution?
3. What method of execution is the most barbaric? What method is the most humane?
4. What methods have been abolished?

Harold Hillman, "An Unnatural Way to Die," *New Scientist,* October, 1983, pp. 276-78.

In April 1982, John Louis Evans was shocked for half a minute. This broke the leg electrode, which was reattached. A second shock failed to kill him, and smoke was seen coming out of his mouth and his left leg; he was given a third dose. It took 10 minutes before the attending physician certified him as being dead.

Last July, the British parliament voted decisively against the re-introduction of the death penalty, and everyone, it seemed, had an opinion on it. But what happens during an execution? Why does the person die? Is it painful? Is death instantaneous? Which is the most humane method? Here I shall deal with the techniques most commonly used in countries which practice capital punishment. I shall discuss only those methods in which execution is the primary intention, although torture, flogging or starvation of prisoners frequently result in death.

Hanging

If the death penalty had been re-introduced in Britain, hanging would probably have been the method. The prisoner is blindfolded and stands on a trap door, with a rope around his neck. The trap door is opened suddenly. The weight of the prisoner's body below the neck causes traction and tearing of the cervical muscles, skin and blood vessels. The upper cervical vertebrae are dislocated, and the spinal cord is separated from the brain: this is the lesion which causes death. The volume of blood in the skull and face quickly increases, but soon the blood supply to the brain falls drastically (ischaemia). The respiratory and then the heart rate slow until they stop, and death supervenes.

Initially during hanging the prisoner attempts to move, presumably reacting mainly to the pain of neck traction and dislocation. Later on, there is a second series of more theatrical reflex movements, as a result of spinal reflexes originating at the site of severance of the brain from the spinal cord. Contrary to the beliefs of Victorian novelists, the later movements usually occur when the prisoner is unconscious, and are not evidence that he or she can still feel it. It is often thought that hanging immediately arrests respiration and heartbeat; this is wrong. They both *start* to slow immediately, but whereas breathing stops in seconds, the heart may beat for minutes. Blood loss plays little part in death due to hanging.

It is impossible to know for how long the condemned person feels pain, and the standard practice of hooding prevents observation of the face. Animals in an analogous situation often squeak. Their facial muscles go into spasm in a "risus sardonicus", and they close their eyes.

The person being hanged, in addition to suffering cervical pain, probably has an acute headache from the occlusion of his veins and engorgement of cerebral blood vessels; this results from the rope closing off the veins of the neck before occluding the carotid and vertebral arteries. The vertebral and spinal arteries are deep and are protected normally by bone, although this protection may be diminished by the dislocation.

In experiments during the Second World War on human volunteers in the US, in which the pressure at the lower end of the neck was suddenly raised to 600mm mercury, consciousness was lost in 6 to 7 seconds. During this time, there would have been sufficient blood in the brain to maintain consciousness and, therefore, feel pain.

Much of our knowledge of what happens during hanging is derived from observations on animals whose necks have been dislocated to excise organs for biochemical, pharmacological and physiological experiments *in vitro.* This is the commonest method used to "sacrifice" animals when a researcher does not want an experiment influenced by anaesthesia. Of course, the same events occur when a farmer or slaughterer wrings an animal's neck.

Shooting

Shooting is probably the second most widely used technique of execution. Death is virtually instantaneous if the person is shot at close quarters through the skull; the bullet penetrates the medulla, which contains the vital respirator and cardiac centers, among others.

But condemned prisoners are usually shot by firing

squads aiming at the heart from some metres away. As was shown by the assassination attempts on both President Ronald Reagan and on Pope John Paul — but not, alas, on President John F. Kennedy — it is difficult to shoot a person dead with a single or few shots, except at very close range. The reason for this is that the cause of death in these cases is normally blood loss through rupture of the heart or a large blood vessel, or tearing of the lungs. Any lover of grand opera or classical Westerns knows that death in these circumstances takes several minutes, quite enough for the victim to sing a powerful aria or almost to describe the location of the buried treasure.

Persons suffering bullet wounds have reported that they felt as if they had been kicked hard by a horse; they do not always experience severe pain immediately, and they lose consciousness when the shock causes a fall in blood supply to the brain. Firing squads usually kill quickly because a substantial number of soldiers fire simultaneously.

Bullets cause a great deal of damage in tissues by releasing some of their enormous energy. The energy of a particle is a function of the square of its velocity. High-velocity missiles, such as rifle bullets, have a tremendous amount of energy, which is partly released as heat within the tissues. This causes evaporation of the tissues and water to form a carrot-shaped space several hundred times the volume of the original bullet; this phenomenon is called "cavitation". When the bullet has passed through, the cavity collapses, and sucks in dead tissue and contaminated air.

The Guillotine

The guillotine was named after the French deputy who proposed the use of the device in 1789. It was tested on corpses at the Bicetre Hospital in Paris, and employed by the French Revolution in 1792. It was introduced as a swift and painless device — as Joseph-Ignace Guillotin believed — to extend to all citizens the advantages of a technique used only on noblemen in France. Although most people believe that Guillotin invented the device, it had been previously used in Italy, Germany, France and Scotland in the 16th Century.

Guillotining was considered more humane because the

blade was sharper and execution was more rapid than was normally accomplished with an axe. Death occurs due to separation of the brain and spinal cord, after transection of the surrounding tissues. This must cause acute and possibly severe pain. Consciousness is probably lost within 2-3 seconds, due to a rapid fall of intracranial perfusion of blood.

There are accounts in the literature of the eyes looking around from the severed head, and animals may do this when they are guillotined for experiments in which their organs are to be excised or their brain biochemistry is to be examined rapidly.

Garrotting

Garrotting was used in the Iberian Peninsula until about 10 years ago. It is a form of strangulation by a metal collar with a clamp. Those who use it believe that the resultant dislocation of the neck is rapid and death is instantaneous. Unfortunately, although the clamp is tightened very quickly, the degree of compression of the neck sufficient to dislocate it takes some seconds to achieve. The tissues of the neck are tough and the application of the contraption is highly disagreeable. In addition to compressing the soft tissues, the clamp occludes the trachea. Therefore it kills by asphyxia, cerebral ischaemia and neck dislocation. Dying is painful, deeply distressing and may take several minutes.

Electrocution

Electrocution was approved by the state of New York in 1888. Its use was immediately but unsuccessfully challenged in the federal courts as being a "cruel and unusual punishment." But it was used two years later, and several hundred people a year were executed in the US for rape and armed robbery, as well as murder, until the end of the 1960s.

The prisoner is securely fastened to a chair by his chest, groin, arms and legs to prevent violent movements and to keep the electrodes in place. These are moistened copper terminals attached to one calf and a band round the head. "Jolts" of 4-8 amperes at voltages between 500 and 2000 volts are applied for half a minute at a time, and a doctor inspects the condemned man to decide if he is dead, or if another jolt should be administered.

In April 1982, John Louis Evans was shocked for half a minute. This broke the leg electrode, which was re-attached. A second shock failed to kill him, and smoke was seen coming out of his mouth and his left leg; he was given a third dose. It took 10 minutes before the attending physician certified him as being dead.

The Chair awaits a flood of executions.

After an earlier electrocution, at post mortem the temperature of the leg electrode was found to be 54°C — about the temperature of a very hot bath.

Every first-aider is taught that the effects of accidental electrocution are burns, respiratory paralysis and cardiac arrest. The widespread use of the electric chair for execution — like its use for the disposal of unwanted pets — was based on the belief that it caused instantaneous and painless death. In recent years, closer observation and attention have indicated clearly that this is not the case. In fact, there is no reason whatsoever to believe that the condemned person does not suffer severe and prolonged pain. He is so firmly fastened to the chair that he cannot move. The large amount of energy in the shock paralyses his muscles. Presumably it was the failure to move which led to the general belief that the prisoner was not suffering pain. However, it has been known for several decades that lack of movement does not mean absence of pain . . . Indeed, a prisoner being electrocuted is paralysed and asphyxiated, but almost certainly is fully conscious and sentient. He feels himself being burnt to death while he is conscious of his inability to breathe. It must feel very similar to the medieval trial by ordeal of being dropped into boiling oil . . .

Injection and Gassing

In eight States of the Union, condemned persons may have the choice of being killed by **intravenous injection,** by hanging or shooting. On 2 December, 1982, Charlie Brooks of Texas had his vein cannulated by a physician. Then, from outside the execution chamber and unseen by the prisoner, a mixture was injected; this consisted of the rapidly acting anaesthetic pentothal, curare to paralyse the muscles, and potassium chloride to stop the heart . . .

Another eight states have chosen **gassing** as a form of capital punishment. On 2 September, 1983, Jimmy Lee Gray was strapped to a chair in an airtight room. Sodium cyanide crystals were dropped into a bath of sulphuric acid below his chair, by depressing a lever from outside. Hydrogen cyanide gas evolved and the condemned man inhaled it. A sufficient concentration to constitute a lethal dose would take several seconds to minutes to accumulate, depending on how hard he tried to avoid inhaling. It would cause acute difficulty in breathing, asphyxia and, possibly, pain in the stomach. The prisoner would be severely distressed and in pain during the whole procedure. The resultant hypoxia would cause him to have spasms as in an epileptic fit, visible if he were not bound firmly; the strapping would prevent the appearance of spasms, but not their occurrence. The prisoner would have died of inhibition of respiratory enzymes . . .

In this article, I have deliberately not discussed the

morality of capital punishment, since I believe that a physician or a physiologist has no more expertise in general moral and ethical questions than does anyone else. Each citizen should decide for himself whether society should subject a criminal to the short period of pain and distress, as justice for the prolonged and profound pain or distress that he may have caused others. Each citizen also has to consider whether he believes the lives of those who destroy others are as sacred as those who are pillars of society, or whether the destruction of anti-social individuals is a necessary price to pay to protect law-abiding citizens from them.

I have attempted to give what I believe to be the physiological facts of execution. They are inescapable even if gruesome, but, if considered, may well help us to make appropriate moral decisions.

A MORE HUMANE METHOD: THE CASE FOR LETHAL INJECTION

Thomas H. Paterniti

Thomas H. Paterniti is a dentist in Metuchen, New Jersey and an Assemblyman representing District 18 (Middlesex) in the New Jersey State Legislature. He was the author of legislation introducing lethal injection as the method of execution in New Jersey. This legislation was passed by the legislature and signed into law by the Governor.

Points to Consider

1. What is lethal injection?
2. How is lethal injection administered?
3. Why is lethal injection a humane method of execution?
4. What are other advantages of lethal injection?

Excerpted from a statement written for this volume by Thomas H. Paterniti, April 16, 1984.

As long as we have animals in our society who take pleasure in killing or maiming others, we have a right — an obligation to fight back and say no more.

People ask me why I came up with this method and why I feel it's humane. First of all the whole procedure is a very serious matter and a personal one. I wanted it to be as painless as possible because the death penalty would be less subject to criticism as the opponents would have a difficult time claiming it was painful and inhuman. Also I felt that although murder is sinister, we as civilized people would show murderers more compassion than they show

75 Volunteered

A state Department of Corrections panel has selected five people from a group of over 75 volunteers to serve as executioners in carrying out death sentences in New Jersey, officials said yesterday . . .

Hilton said participants are paid $500 each per execution, adding that they would be paid in cash to avoid a paper trail in the state bureaucracy that might reveal their names . . .

Three drugs will be administered to condemned prisoners: one to cause loss of consciousness, a second to halt breathing, and a third to stop the heart beat.

Two executioners and an alternate will participate in each procedure. They will not be told which of them is administering the lethal mixture and which a harmless saline solution, he said.

The condemned person will be separated from the executioners by a wall, he said.

"The executioners will not see or be seen by either the witnesses or condemned," he said. "They will enter a syringe into an already established (intravenous) line."

Home News, New Brunswick, New Jersey, May 15, 1984.

The Needle

their victims.

My legislation provides that executions in New Jersey under the recently enacted death penalty be carried out by using a lethal injection.

It is designed to carry out an execution in the most humane way possible. It should also satisfy the views of Governor Thomas Kean who has urged that the death penalty be implemented by injection of a lethal drug instead of electrocution.

In my proposal, a condemned person would first be tranquilized or anesthetized by either an oral tablet, capsule or an intra-muscular injection of a narcotic or barbituate prior to the actual injection of the lethal solution.

The measure also requires that the procedures and equipment used to administer the lethal solution be carried out in "such a way that the identity of the person actually inflicting the fatal injection be unknown even to himself".

This could be done by having a number of persons involved in the execution process which could be triggered by computer or other mechanical means.

Medical Groups

To circumvent the reluctance expressed by medical groups of having doctors administer the fatal injection, my legislation establishes a category of "execution technicians". The category would be filled by persons designated by the Commissioner of Corrections. They would be familiar with medical procedures and would be qualified to administer injections.

The method of execution advocated in my bill has the backing of Dr. Howard Slobodien, who is president of the New Jersey Medical Association.

To reduce the "carnival atmosphere" surrounding an execution, my legislation would limit those present at the event to the commissioner, two physicians, execution

---

More Humane

New Jersey's proposed method of executing convicted murderers "shows more compassion" than the lethal injection method used to put murder convict Charlie Brooks Jr. to death in Texas, the author of New Jersey's lethal injection legislation said yesterday . . .

Paterniti said he was bothered by the fact that Brooks experienced pain during the execution.

"My bill would eliminate that. Anyone executed in New Jersey would be anesthetized first and then given the lethal injection after the anesthesia took effect," he explained.

"I think there would be no discomfort at all for the person being executed in New Jersey. Our method would be much more humane if that can be the case in an execution," he said . . .

Paterniti said he believed other states would use New Jersey's lethal injection legislation as a "model" once the procedure becomes law.

The Woodbridge, N.J. *News Tribune,* December 8, 1982.

technicians and two members of the clergy. Also six members of the news media and six witnesses.

To forestall delays, the legislation further requires that the date of execution be set within 30 to 60 days of the issuance of the death warrant by the presiding judge.

I feel this is good legislation because it tries to bring a degree of humaneness to a very difficult subject.

Sure it would be nice not to have a need for the death penalty, but as long as we have animals in our society who take pleasure in killing or maiming others, we have a right — an obligation to fight back and say no more.

IDEAS IN CONFLICT

TOWARD A MORE CIVILIZED BARBARISM: THE CASE AGAINST LETHAL INJECTION

Colman McCarthy

Colman McCarthy is a syndicated writer and columnist. The following article deals with his objections to the death penalty and the notion that a humane form of execution can ever be used.

Points to Consider

1. What problems have resulted during executions?
2. Why is lethal injection barbaric?
3. What did Ronald Reagan say about lethal injection?
4. What could talk of "humane executions" lead to?

Drugs do not induce the "quick and painless" deaths the new humanitarians say they will. Along with defective electric chairs, recalls for drugs may be in order, give or take a few lives.

Penal officials in New Jersey, backed by the state Legislature, are deciding that the humane way to execute prisoners is by lethal intravenous injection. By killing them with kindness, New Jersey's executioners reject such harsher, unworkmanlike methods as electrocution, hanging, shooting and gassing.

Mercy and Efficiency

The occasion for this decision was the death sentence imposed in May on a twice-convicted murderer. New Jersey, which had killed 160 men and women in the electric chair before a 10-year execution respite beginning in 1972, restored the death penalty last year. It will become the ninth state to allow injections.

A New York Times story told of an assistant to the governor who recently spent eight months researching the technology of legalized death. He was persuaded to recommend injections after reading a law journal article that detailed the botchings that can occur when, say, a firing squad doesn't aim straight and misses the heart.

Other screw-ups have occurred. In Alabama last April, a malfunctioning electric chair meant that three surges of 1,900 volts were needed to kill a condemned prisoner. One surge usually does it, but on this occasion, with 34 reporters watching the action, a leather strap holding an electrode on the man's left leg burned away. Fourteen minutes of sparks, smoke and flames — hellfire on death row — passed between the first jolt and the doctor's pronouncement of death.

Without the benefit of a national recall for defective electric chairs, New Jersey officials are demanding efficiency as well as mercy. "Execution technicians" are to be trained. With steady hands that can wield the needle

More Obscene

This new method of execution has occasioned more controversy than it deserves. The question remains not how executions should be done but rather whether they should be done at all. The answer is no.

Gov. James Thompson recently vetoed a proposed change in Illinois's method of execution from the electric chair to lethal injection, explaining that opponents of capital punishment would not be mollified by a different method and that supporters of the death penalty could rely on the effectiveness of electrocution. He was quite right. For those of us who oppose the death penalty, execution is the crime for which it purports to be the punishment: it is a homicide, no matter how lawful and whatever the method . . .

The method used in our official and ceremonious homicides is ultimately a negligible issue. But lethal injection may be more obscene because it provides the illusion of humaneness in the killing.

Henry Schwarzchild, American Civil Liberties Union, 1982.

under pressure, they won't be likely to repeat the Alabama thriller.

It Is Never Humane

New Jersey's penologists are seeking to edge away from barbarity. They are really hurtling closer to it.

They are not only taking lives but are enshrouding the process in the lie that planned killing can somehow, with the proper laying on of trained hands, be humane. Whether it's a gangland murder by thugs or a death-row killing sanctioned by the governor, taking a life coldbloodedly is always an act of horror and terror.

In the history of capital punishment in American prisons, every new technique has been hailed as more humane than the last. Electrocution was said to be better than shooting, which was better than hanging. Then gassing had a vogue.

One of the first politicians to urge death-by-drugs as a

humanitarian advance was none other than Ronald Reagan.

In 1973, when governor of California, he said: "Being a former farmer and horse raiser, I know what it's like to try to eliminate an injured horse by shooting him. Now you call the veterinarian and the vet gives it a shot and the horse goes to sleep — that's it. I myself have wondered if maybe this isn't

part of our problem (with capital punishment), and maybe we should review and see if there aren't even more humane methods now — the simple shot or tranquilizer."

Reagan's yearning for a simpler way of killing horses and people has proven to be as dotty and unfounded as his yearning for a simpler America. A current suit before the U.S. Court of Appeals in the District of Columbia, brought on behalf of eight prisoners condemned to die in Oklahoma and Texas, raises the question of whether the drugs perform as well as they should.

Affidavits from anesthesiologists stated that untested and unapproved drugs are used in lethal injections. The suit asks that the Food and Drug Administration hold hearings to gather evidence — if any exists — that the drugs are effective.

The current state of the grisly art suggests the opposite — that the drugs do not induce the "quick and painless" deaths the new humanitarians say they will. Along with defective electric chairs, recalls for drugs may be in order, give or take a few lives.

Easy Death

In New Jersey, it came out that concern for the condemned was not the total story. An assemblyman pushing drugs as the ideal pain-killing killing agent had the comfort of juries also on his mind: "If you're on the jury, the thought of some guy in that chair sizzling is going to bother them. This way, with lethal injections, it might ease their conscience when they come up with a verdict."

Talk of easy death and easy verdicts may extend into the killing chamber itself. The last words from the "execution technician" could be the time-honored ones of medicine, "Just relax, you won't feel a thing."

That lie will be the next-to-last brutality from the state.

PHYSICIANS HAVE ALWAYS PARTICIPATED

George J. Annas, J.D., M.P.H.

George J. Annas has a law degree and a Masters Degree in Public Health. He is a frequent contributor to Medicolegal News *and has written numerous articles on medical ethics. In this article, he deals with the relationship of physicians to the death penalty.*

Points to Consider

1. What has been the traditional role of physicians in executions?
2. In what ways should physicians be associated with the death penalty?
3. Why was Gary Gilmore's execution significant for doctors?
4. What "new dimensions" have been added to the death penalty by the use of lethal injection as a method of execution?

George J. Annas, "Doctors and the Death Penalty," *Medicolegal News,* April, 1980.

The fact is that physicians have always participated in an active way in the infliction of the death penalty, and have traditionally brought their medical knowledge and training to bear on the process.

Proponents of the death penalty have shifted gears. In the past, gruesome public executions were extolled as a deterrent to others, and even in recent times, death has been inflicted on convicted criminals by hanging, firing squads, electrocution and poisonous gas. All of these methods inflict pain on the victim and have the potential for failure and added suffering — both physical and mental. Many have argued that they are all potentially or actually "cruel and unusual" punishment, and a series of United States Supreme Court decisions suggests that this may be so.

Defenders of the death penalty, however, do not give up easily; and the current search is for a "humane" way to continue executions. Recently, four states have passed statutes embodying this "humane" alternative. In the words of the New Mexico statute:

> The manner of inflicting the punishment of death shall be by administration of a continuous intravenous injection of a lethal quantity of an ultra-short-acting barbiturate in combination with a chemical paralytic agent.

Even critics of the death penalty have conceded that death would come with "minimal violence, no mutilation, and little more indignity than an ordinary surgical procedure," and that it is "clearly the most humane of the present methods."

A New Dimension

To some, however, a new dimension has been added to the death penalty question by making the physician the instrument of death — either by having him order the injection or actually administer it. The argument is that medical ethics "should be interpreted to unconditionally condemn medical participation in this new form of capital punishment." The rationale for condemning injections but not the former modes of death dealing is that injection presents "a more obvious application of biomedical knowledge and skills than any other method of execution yet adopted by any other nation in modern history." While I have much sympathy for the argument, I do not think it is tenable. The fact is that physicians have always participated in an active way in the infliction of the death penalty, and have traditionally brought their medical knowledge and training to bear on the process. The mere fact that the actual instrument of death

---

Nothing New

There is nothing new about medical participation in state executions. Doctors have been present at and have had roles in official executions for centuries. The guillotine was invented by a dedicated physician and social reformer who opposed the death penalty; the invention was thought to be a more humane method of killing. In this country in 1887 a commission of physicians opposed execution by hanging because of its frequent bungling and resultant prolonged suffering and because it lowered the dignity of the law by its public spectacle. The commission recommended more humane forms of killing, including electrocution, cyanide poisoning, chloroform overdosing, and intravenous injection of morphine. They favored electrocution over the chemical methods. Thomas Edison supported the use of electricity for electrocutions.

Ward Cassells, M.D., The New England Journal of Medicine, January 24, 1980.

---

can now be seen by everyone as "medical" does not change the moral or ethical (or legal for that matter) considerations: it just makes them easier to appreciate.

Physicians, for example, are always present to pronounce death; and this involves much more than just that act. It is only *after* the physician has pronounced the "patient" dead that he can be cut down if the method is hanging, taken out of the gas chanber if it is poisonous gas, or taken out of the electric chair in the case of electrocution. The death of Gary

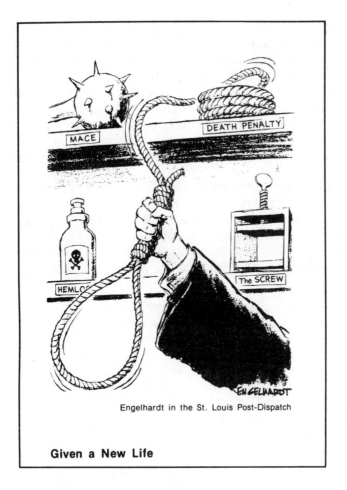

Engelhardt in the St. Louis Post-Dispatch

Given a New Life

Gilmore by firing squad provides a scenario of the doctor's active participation in this "traditional" mode. Norman Mailer describes the scene as the doctor pinned a white circle on Gary's black shirt as a target for the firing squad. After the shots penetrated his body and blood began dripping on the floor, "The doctor came along with a stethoscope and shook his head. Gilmore wasn't dead yet . . . they waited about twenty seconds. Then the doctor went up again . . . and nodded."

A Meaningful Distinction

It does not seem to me that a meaningful distinction can

be made between the physician who orders the mixture of drugs that will be injected into a prisoner's body, and the physician who pins the target over the prisoner's heart and uses his skills to declare the prisoner dead. It surely makes no moral difference whether or not the physician uses his stethoscope as an instrument to pronounce death; nor does it make a legal or ethical difference whether he pins a target on the prisoner or prepares a lethal injection. It is the nature of the action and its intent, not the nature of the instrument used, that is the crucial factor.

Capital punishment should be condemned in *all* forms as an act which itself is inhumane no matter what the method of execution is. Worrying about whether or not physicians should get more directly involved misses the central issue in the death penalty debate and drains off energy and thought which should be mobilized toward ending the death penalty once and for all.

5 READING

DOCTORS MUST NOT TAKE PART

American Medical Association

This statement was taken from Current Opinions of the Judicial Council of the American Medical Association. *It was made in response to the debate that has arisen in regard to the role doctors should play in executions by lethal injections and other methods as well. Lethal injection presents a more direct application of medical knowledge than other methods of execution and has promoted an international debate.*

Points to Consider

1. What stand does the American Medical Association take on the death penalty?
2. How have doctors reacted to the use of lethal injection?
3. Should physicians play any role in executions?
4. What recommendations does the American Medical Association make?

Statement by the Judicial Council of the American Medical Association, 1984.

Whatever conclusions on methods of capital punishment that society may have reached through its elected representatives in the legislature, the active participation by physicians in executions is not required.

Since the start of this year, the Judicial Council has received a variety of inquiries from individual physicians and medical societies on physician involvement with capital punishment. Four states have recently passed legislation authorizing capital punishment by intravenous injection of lethal substances. No executions have, in fact, been performed under such statutes. None of the statutes requires a physician to inject the toxic substance.

Individual physician response to this method of execution has been more emotive than conclusive. Some physicians have favored such proposals; others have opposed them. Much of the discussion has turned on whether capital punishment itself is supported or opposed. Not surprisingly, those favoring capital punishment tend to support such legislation, while those opposing capital punishment do not.

Debate over capital punishment has occurred for centuries and remains a volatile social, political, and legal issue in our own time. The Judicial Council doubts that this report will resolve this debate, nor does the Council intend this report to do so. The rightness or wrongness of capital punishment is a personal moral decision that each individual in our society must personally resolve. The concern of this report is limited to a question of professional responsibility and decision-making, viz., active participation by physicians in capital punishment.

The Debate

Those arguing in favor of capital punishment by drug injection assert that it is more humane and less painful than other methods. Historical examples, such as the development of the guillotine by two French physicians or a 19th century American physicians' study favoring electrocution or drug overdose to hanging, are typically cited as examples of medical involvement with recommendations for more humane methods of execution. Those favoring death by injection also assert that it is less likely to be subject to social or legal objection and that it wll be less expensive than other methods. If medical technicians are used, physicians need not be actively involved in administering the drug or participating in the execution.

Those arguing against this method of execution assert that it manipulates the profession into a position condoning capital punishment, even though physicians are trained to save life, not take it. Physicians are not trained to administer drug overdoses, nor is it typically contemplated within the practice of medicine. If medical technicians are used, a physician may still be involved with prescribing the drug or supervising the injection. Finally, the contrary argument goes, physician participation projects a poor public image.

The Judicial Council imagines that all of the above, pro and con, may be true. The factor that predominates, however, is that professional standards in medicine always rest on the most fundamental of concepts, "primum non nocere," above all do no harm. It is harmful to take a life. Regardless of one's personal moral decision on capital punishment, professional decisions are always tempered by this concern. Knowledge of our capabilities in pharmacology, toxicology, catheterization, or injection do not require the services of a physician in this setting. Whatever conclusions on methods of capital punishment that society

Making Doctors Executioners

An insidious aberration is being added to the American lunge back toward capital punishment. Some state legislatures would, in effect, turn physicians into executioners by specifying that the condemned be killed by the injection of drugs. Part of the reasoning is that this "humane" method of execution might make restoration of the death penalty more acceptable. The echoes of Hitler's perversion of medicine for state purposes are too abhorrent to be ignored.

The Christian Science Monitor, February 28, 1980.

IT'S THE GOVERNOR......

Reprinted with permission of the *Minneapolis Star and Tribune*

may have reached through its elected representatives in the legislature, the active participation by physicians in executions is not required.

As a final point, those opposing death by injection have claimed that a physician should not even be available to certify the death of the executed individual. In the rare instances when capital punishment occurs in this country by other methods, a physician could and would presumably be available to declare that the individual was dead. This determination has not traditionally been considered to constitute professional sanction (or disapproval) of capital punishment. A pronouncement of death is, rather, legally required by a designated class of individuals (typically physicians) under state law so that public records may certify to the fact of death. This is true in all instances of death, not just death by execution. Certification of death by a physician is not a part of the act of execution and is not, therefore, improper.

Conclusion

The Judicial Council recommends that the House of Delegates adopt the following:
1. An individual's opinion on capital punishment is the

personal moral decision of the individual.

2. A physician, as a member of a profession dedicated to preserving life when there is hope of doing so, should not be a participant in a legally authorized execution.

3. A physician may make a determination or certification of death as currently provided by law in any situation.

6 READING

IDEAS IN CONFLICT

EXECUTIONS SHOULD
NOT BE EASY

The News and Courier

This statement was taken from an editorial in **The News and
Courier** *of Charleston, South Carolina. The editors argue that
executions should be terrible and dreadful, rather than
humane. Executions then are rituals and social symbols that
help explain the sacredness of human life.*

Points to Consider

1. Who was Charlie Brooks and how was he executed?
2. Why is the "humaneness" of lethal injection so
frightening?
3. Why should execution be terrible and dreadful?
4. What is the social role of executions?

Reprinted from an editorial in *The News and Courier* newspaper of
Charleston, South Carolina, December 21, 1982.

The power of execution as a means of safeguarding society from murderers rests in its very terribleness.

If capital punishment is to have the awesome effectiveness sought by society, it should be accompanied by capital justice. Unfortunately, the recent execution of convicted murderer Charlie Brooks Jr. in Huntsville, Texas, climaxed a judicial process which was just the opposite of capital.

Never Carried Out

By now it has occurred to many that the truly "cruel and inhuman" aspect of the death penalty is the fact that, once imposed, it almost never is carried out.

Reinforcing that conclusion is the last-minute reprieve from a lethal drug injection of a convicted murderer in Texas. Needles already had been inserted when word came that Supreme Court Justice Byron White had issued a stay . . .

The death penalty as presently hamstrung by the Supreme Court is a farce. It mocks the efforts of prosecutors, judges and juries in fulfilling their responsibilities. An aroused citizenry should demand prompt remedial action by the court and Congress.

The Daily Oklahoman, editorial, October 7, 1983.

Consider the contradictions and unhappy symbolism in the first execution carried out by lethal injection.

Brooks was executed despite the pleas of Jack Strickland, who, as prosecutor, originally convinced jurors to apply the death penalty. Mr. Strickland fought up to the eleventh hour to secure a reprieve for Brooks because he was not convinced that the man about to be executed was the murderer. Brooks was convicted on the basis of the evidence provided by another man, also charged with the murder. Although it is

not known which of the men pulled the trigger, Brooks' accomplice received a 40-year sentence on a plea-bargain. Strickland made this worrying comment, "It may well be, as horrible as it is to contemplate, that the state of Texas executed the wrong man . . ."

As if that were not enough, there are several other aspects of the execution which will provide ammunition for those people who are utterly opposed to capital punishment. At a time when those campaigning for its abolition are arguing that advocates of execution are racially motivated, the first convicted murderer to receive an injection of Sodium Pentothal, which is a controversial method of taking life, happens to be black.

The method used to execute Brooks is chilling because it reminds us that we are only a little over a year away from 1984, the date George Orwell chose for his novel about the horror of the totalitarian police state. The very "humaneness" of lethal injection is what makes it so frightening. It is precisely the method that "Big Brother" would choose.

Symbolism of Executions

The symbolism surrounding an execution should not be that associated with doctors, with good bedside manners, who assure their patients that "this is not going to hurt." The power of execution as a means of safeguarding society from murderers rests in its very terribleness. An execution says to society that it is a very dreadful thing to take the life of another human being. Execution is the ultimate penalty, which must only be applied after a fair trial and with all the majesty of justice. An execution is not merely a way of putting people away "humanely" — like putting down a savage animal — it is a message about the sacredness of human life. The death penalty is effective only when it is seen as an act of last resort, a final sorrowing act of society. That is why methods of execution have always been traditionally horrible. They are not, as some people would argue, acts of barbarism. They are rituals. They are not meant to rid society of its scum, but cleanse it. The worrying thing about an execution by injection is not that it provides an easy death for the victim but that it provides society with an easy way of disposing of victims. If an execution were to give no pain to society, we could live to rue the day when people are "put to sleep" like animals. Execution is a matter of exception and it should always remain so. It should be carried out in the presence of those representatives of society responsible

---

Real Easy

Three executioners would stand behind a partitioned wall, each holding a syringe. Two contain a harmless sugar solution and the third contains the lethal drug.

The syringe plungers are pressed and the condemned person is quickly executed by a massive barbiturate overdose.

One prison official, who worked on an oldtime death row, put it like this:

"The guy will just go to sleep forever. It will be easy — real easy."

Corrections Digest, **October 14, 1977.**

for the decision. We should not make it easy for society to execute. Execution must be seen as society's act of last resort when, after a fair trial, it is decided by a jury that the circumstances of a particular murder demand the ultimate penalty. Justice must be applied in all its dreadful majesty.

ALL EXECUTIONS ARE BARBARIC

John G. Healey

John G. Healey is the executive director of Amnesty International, USA. His article is a response to the national concern and debate over humane executions and lethal injection as a painless method of execution. He believes that all executions violate the sacredness of life.

Points to Consider

1. What is the purpose of Amnesty International?
2. How does the author describe the death penalty in foreign nations?
3. Why are all executions the same?
4. Why isn't there a humane way to execute?

John G. Healey, "There is No Humane Way to Kill," *Amnesty Action,* March, 1983.

Those who have experienced mock execu-
tions — such as the US hostages in Iran —
can testify that there is no humane way to
kill.

Amnesty International works to protect the most fundamental of human rights - those limits on a government's
power over the individual which have been enshrined in the
Universal Declaration of Human Rights: the right not to be
arrested simply for one's beliefs, religion, or race; the right
to receive a prompt and fair trial; and, finally, the right in all
cases and under all circumstances not to be subjected to
torture or cruel, inhuman or degrading treatment or punishment. It is this last right that we wish to focus on today.

The need for Americans to discuss the prohibition against
torture and cruel, inhuman and degrading punishment is
urgent, for the violation of this right is not restricted to nations abroad. One need look no further than the State of
Virginia, which last August killed a man by electrocution.
And one need look no later than yesterday, [January 23]
when the State of Texas came within hours of repeating last
month's pioneer use of medicine to kill through the injection
of a lethal dosage of poison. More than a thousand men and
women in prison throughout the United States wait for
similar acts to be performed on them.

A Select Group of Nations

In allowing such killings to be carried out by its State
governments, the United States joins a select group of nations of approximately 30 which in the past year are making
active use of the death penalty. In fact, of the NATO countries, only the United States and Turkey still use the death
penalty.

The crimes for which the death penalty is imposed and
the procedures by which it is carried out, of course, vary
greatly from nation to nation. In the Soviet Union, people are
killed for economic crimes, and in Yemen for political
crimes; in South Africa, those who are executed belong
almost exclusively to one race; in China, the executions are
carried out after mass rallies; in Iran, after a few minutes

before a revolutionary court; and in Guatemala, the few legal executions are far exceeded by government killings taking place in the street, completely outside the judicial process. Certainly few other countries on the list can match the legal protections offered by the US judicial system.

Inhuman and Degrading

And yet, in the most fundamental sense, all executions

Barbarousness

The classic form of execution, still in use in several states, is hanging. Ideally, the neck will be broken, but if the drop is too short there will be a slow and agonizing death by strangulation. If the drop is too long the head will be torn off.

The first major substitute for hanging was electrocution, the most widely used form of execution in this country. The condemned prisoner is led — or dragged — into the death chamber, strapped into the chair, and electrodes fastened to head and legs. When the switch is thrown the body strains, jolting as the voltage is raised and lowered. Often smoke rises from the head. There is the awful odor of burning flesh. No one knows how long electrocuted individuals retain consciousness.

An attempt to improve on electrocution was the gas chamber. The prisoner is strapped into a chair, a container of sulphuric acid underneath. The chamber is sealed and cyanide is dropped into the acid to form lethal gas. As the gas fills the chamber, the prisoner turns purple and drools. The eyes pop. Unconsciousness may not come for several minutes, but even then the body continues to struggle for air . . .

Most people observing an execution are horrified and disgusted. Revulsion at the duty to supervise and witness executions is one reason why so many prison wardens, people unsentimental about crime and criminals, are opponents of capital punishment.

Hugo A. Bedau, *Against the Death Penalty,* 1977.

are the same. In each case a government has decided that it has the right to remove a selected individual not merely from society but from life itself. In each case the method is cruel, inhuman and degrading. Those who have experienced mock executions — such as the US hostages in Iran — can testify that there is no humane way to kill.

Those working against the death penalty in the United States appear to be faced with an increasingly difficult, if not hopeless, task. Working against the death penalty on a worldwide basis — as Amnesty International does — besides the many reasons for concern, also offers hope.

RECOGNIZING AUTHOR'S POINT OF VIEW

This activity may be used as an individualized study guide for students in libraries and resource centers or as a discussion catalyst in small group and classroom discussions.

The capacity to recognize an author's point of view is an essential reading skill. Many readers do not make clear distinctions between descriptive articles that relate factual information and articles that express a point of view. Think about the readings in chapter two. Are these readings essentially descriptive articles that relate factual information or articles that attempt to persuade through editorial commentary and analysis?

Guidelines

1. The following are brief descriptions of sources that appeared in chapter two. Choose one of the following source descriptions that best defines each source in chapter two.

Source Descriptions

a. Essentially an article that relates factual information
b. Essentially an article that expresses editorial points of view
c. Both of the above
d. Neither of the above

Sources in Chapter Two

_____ Source One
"Methods of Execution: The Medical and Biological Effects," by Harold Hillman.

_____ Source Two
"A More Humane Method: The Case for Lethal Injection," by Thomas H. Paterniti.

_____ Source Three
"Toward a More Civilized Barbarism: The Case
Against Lethal Injection," by Colman McCarthy.

_____ Source Four
"Physicians Have Always Participated," by George
J. Annas.

_____ Source Five
"Doctors Must Not Take Part," by the American
Medical Association.

_____ Source Six
"Executions Should Not Be Easy," by _The News
and Courier_ in Charleston, South Carolina.

_____ Source Seven
"All Executions Are Barbaric," by John G. Healey.

2. Summarize the author's point of view in one to three
sentences for each of the readings in chapter two.

3. After careful consideration, pick out one reading that you
think is the most reliable source. Be prepared to explain
the reasons for your choice in a general class discussion.

CHAPTER 3

THE DEATH PENALTY:
PRO AND CON

8

POINT

CAPITAL PUNISHMENT DOES NOT DETER

Howard Zehr

Howard Zehr is director of the Mennonite Central Committee U.S. Office of Criminal Justice. This statement was excerpted from a pamphlet published jointly by the Mennonite Central Committee U.S. Office of Criminal Justice and the Victims Offender Ministries Program of the Mennonite Central Committee in Canada.

Points to Consider

1. How can the death penalty cause more violence?
2. What arguments are presented against the deterrence theory?
3. What is the real social message of the death penalty?
4. What do statistics say about murderers?

Howard Zehr, "Death as a Penalty," pamphlet by the Mennonite Central Committee of the U.S. and Canada, 1984.

Rather than preventing violence, capital punishment may have a "brutalizing effect" that increases the level of violence in society. It may raise, not lower, murder rates.

We are scared. Surveys find that the fear of crime is high and perhaps rising. So the question of prevention is important.

General deterrence is the idea that punishing an offender "deters" others from committing similar crimes. But does the threat of the death penalty actually discourage others from killing and thus make it safer? If so, does it do so significantly better than other forms of punishment?

Dozens of studies have examined the relationship between murder and the death penalty in Canada, the United States and elsewhere. They have compared murder rates in areas with the death penalty to those in areas without the death penalty. They examined what happened to murder rates when the death penalty was added or removed in various areas and countries.

None of these studies, however, has been able to establish that the death penalty results in lower murder rates or that the abolition of the death penalty increases murder rates.

If the death penalty deters, the deterrent effect is so small that even the most sophisticated attempts have been unable to measure it.

The vast preponderance of evidence suggests that the death penalty is no more effective than imprisonment at deterring others from committing violent crime.

It is not surprising, therefore, that when Canada abolished the death penalty in 1976, substituting mandatory minimum prison sentences, the homicide rate did not rise and in fact may have fallen somewhat. This pattern also has been observed in France and elsewhere.

Actually, the death penalty may have an effect that is the opposite of what is intended. After John Spenkelink was executed in Florida, homicides seemed to rise, and observers have noted the same phenomena in other circumstances.

Recent studies have begun to substantiate that pattern. One study in New York suggests that an execution will result in two or three extra homicides in the following months within that state alone, and possibly more in the entire country.

Rather than preventing violence, capital punishment may have a "brutalizing effect" that increases the level of violence in our society. It may raise, not lower, murder rates.

How could the threat of death fail to prevent — and possibly even cause — violence? To understand this phenomena, we must look at the theory of general deterrence, especially as it relates to the death penalty.

The idea of deterrence assumes that:

1. Each of us decides our actions by weighing the cost of these actions against the benefits. When the cost — in this case the threat of death — outweighs the potential benefits, we are discouraged from committing crimes. Crime is the result of conscious, rational choices.
2. People have a good idea of costs and a high degree of certainty that they will suffer the costs.
3. The consequences are seen as a significant cost at the time of the act.
4. A potential offender identifies with those being punished.

Bad Company

The House of Commons has refused to reinstate the death penalty in Britain, leaving the Soviet Union, South Africa, Japan and the United States as the only industrialized countries that officially put people to death . . .

The action of the Commons left the United States exposed in generally bad company . . .

Tom Wicker, *The New York Times*, 1983.

These assumptions of deterrence theory fail to take into account the nature and meaning of interpersonal violence. They are often unrealistic when applied to the death penalty.

Lets examine these assumptions.

(1) Some crimes, such as tax evasion, involve considerable rational planning and deterrence may have relevance to them. What we know about murder, however, indicates that most homicides are acts of passion, impulsive acts committed under tremendous stress and/or the influence of alcohol or drugs by individuals prone to aggressive, impulsive behavior. These people do not make rational calculations of pain and gain at the time of their acts.

There are, of course, some carefully planned, premeditated murders. However, people committing these murders usually do not expect to be caught. They do not identify with the person "dumb enough" to get caught and convicted, or they decide that the risks of committing murder are worth the benefit.

However, to say that most people murder irrationally is not to say that their violence is completely capricious, without a purpose or logic of its own in the mind of the perpetrator. Many acts of violence are a distorted way of asserting one's sense of self-worth or of getting recognition. As one former armed robber has said, "At least with a shotgun in my hand I was somebody."

(2) To be deterred, a potential offender needs to know the cost of his or her crimes and the likelihood that he or she will suffer these costs. Yet this is almost impossible to calculate. Few murderers are caught, prosecuted, sentenced and actually executed. From the 1930s to the 1960s, when executions were frequent, less than one execution occurred for every 70 murders. In 1979, one person was sentenced to death for every hundred murders, a rate of 1 percent. So it is impossible for a potential killer to know the risks. Yet knowledge and certainty of cost is a key assumption of deterrence theory.

To make the cost of murder certain, we would have to quickly and automatically execute convicted murderers, regardless of circumstances. To apply the death penalty in such a way, we would need to abolish most of the procedural safeguards and constitutional rights we now have. We would have to be willing to execute some innocent people that these safeguards protect. We would have to be willing to increase the chances for the misuse of our legal system. We would have to opt for a justice system without room for mercy, without the possibility of considering circumstances and individuals.

(3) For deterrence to work, the potential offender must see the penalty as a significant threat. But some people commit murder as a way of punishing themselves or of committing suicide. Others see it as a way to gain notoriety. For them, the consequence is an attraction. This may explain in part why executions encourage some homicides and why some convicted killers have asked to die.

(4) But there is an additional reason:

The real message of the death penalty is the legitimacy of lethal violence.

Some potential killers see executions as evidence that lethal vengeance is justified. Instead of identifying with the offender who was caught and executed, they identify with the executioner. They learn from these executions that it is acceptable to eliminate someone who wrongs them, that violence is justified against the deserving. One study has concluded that the atmosphere of violence surrounding an execution encourages someone who has reached "a state of readiness to kill" to translate this attitude into action.

Many argue that a primary function of the death penalty is to communicate the message that killing is taboo. Certainly we need to make that statement, and strongly. But other ways may be more effective. The example of a life for a life may actually cheapen life, not increase its value.

Because these assumptions about the deterrent effect of the death penalty are inaccurate, the death penalty has offered us a false sense of security. And we are left with a series of moral dilemmas:

Can we bear the moral weight of taking a life when the effect is so miniscule that we cannot measure it, and for an effect that we can have, at least as effectively, by alternatives short of death?

Leo Alford was on death row for six years. His sentence was commuted in 1979 to life imprisonment without possibility of parole. An appeal challenging his conviction is still pending.

*Can we take a life when our action may actually en-
courage violence?*
*Even if the death penalty did deter, do we have the
moral right to take the life of one person hoping that we
might possibly deter another person?*

Specific deterrence refers to the fact that executing a
known offender prevents that person from killing again, "deterring" at least that specific offender.

Preventing the recurrence of murder is certainly a serious
concern. Families of murder victims wrestle with this issue,
as we all must.

*Although death incapacitates, it does so at a high
social and moral cost.*
Alternative ways of restraining offenders do exist.
And not all offenders require permanent restraint.

There are dangerous people who must be restrained on a
long-term basis. Under the current law, some of these individuals are released too early, a legitimate cause for
concern.

Statistics reveal that many murderers commit the crime
only once in a lifetime. Such murders happen under extreme
pressure and abnormal circumstances and are unlikely to be
repeated. Statistically, people convicted of murder are
among the most unlikely to commit violent crimes again,
either inside or outside prisons. Prison wardens often
observe that murderers are among the easiest prisoners to
handle.

Moreover, some murderers genuinely do reform. Provisions are needed to take such transformations into account.

The death penalty incapacitates, but so can imprisonment
for those who need long-term restraint. Legal changes are
needed to help sort out those who require such restraint and
to ensure restraint for those who need it, but imprisonment
can protect society effectively.

The questions are whether the death penalty prevents
murders significantly better than imprisonment does and
whether any possible advantage outweighs the substantial
costs.

COUNTERPOINT

THE DEATH PENALTY
PREVENTS CRIME

Norman Darwick

*Norman Darwick made the following statement as the direc-
tor of the International Association of Chiefs of Police in
Gaitherburg, Maryland. This statement is excerpted from
testimony before the Senate Committee on the Judiciary.*

Points to Consider

1. What arguments are presented in favor of the deterrence
theory?
2. What statistics does he use?
3. How does the author counter the most frequent arguments against capital punishment?
4. Who is helped most by the death penalty?

Excerpted from testimony by Norman Darwick before the Senate
Committee on the Judiciary, April 27, 1981.

The more systematically we eliminate murderers by executions, the greater will be the reinforcement against killing and the greater the number of innocent lives saved.

I would like to voice a belief regarding the general nature of capital punishment and its influence on the commission of capital crimes. At the onset, I would like to set forth the association's position on capital punishment. The association favors the imposition of the death penalty for premeditated murder, murder committed during the perpetration of felonies and the killing of law enforcement officers and correctional officials while performing their duties. We strongly believe that capital punishment is a deterrent to the commission of certain crimes, particularly premeditated murder, murder committed during the perpetration of felonies and the killing of law enforcement officers and prison guards. Although the number of incidents in which capital punishment has been exercised has been extremely limited, its total impact as a deterrent to crime has far exceeded its numerical size.

The seriousness of your task and the very great difficulty it poses for you is emphasized by the fact that persons of differing opinions can look at the same basic facts and come to entirely contrary conclusions.

I am sure that most persons who appear before this committee urging legislation to abolish capital punishment do so because of a concern for human life. It is precisely for this reason that I urge the committee to decide in favor of recommending a retention of this form of crime prevention.

The logic which urges an abolition of the death penalty in the interest of human life is more apparent than real. For I am convinced that ultimately abolition of capital punishment would result in a much greater loss of human life than would its retention.

It is admittedly tragic whenever the state in the most awesome exercise of its authority decides that capital punishment must be invoked. Tragic because any loss of human life is a tragedy. But I submit to you that even in the tragedy of human death there are degrees and that it is much more tragic for the innocent to lose his or her life than for the state to take the life of a criminal convicted of a capital offense.

My statement implies a belief that there is a direct relationship between the legal existence of capital punishment and the incidents of criminal homicide. Although statistics are generally unreliable in this area, I am convinced that such a relationship does exist. I am convinced that many potential murderers are deterred simply by their knowledge that capital punishment exists, and may be their fate if they commit the crime they contemplate.

Statistics

I think it significant that during recent years we have seen a consistent reduction in the number of incidents of capital punishment and at the same time a very great increase in the number of criminal homicides. As an example, in 1950, 82 convicted felons were executed, a very great percentage of whom were guilty of the crime of homicide. During the same year, 7,020 criminal homicides were reported.

A decade later, the number of executions dropped to 56 and the number of criminal homicides rose to 9,140. Throughout the 1960s, we experienced a steady increase in the number of criminal homicides with 14,590 recorded in 1969. During the same decade, we saw a practical end to the utilization of the death penalty. Between 1967 and 1977, no executions occurred in the United States, and there were only two in 1967 and one execution in 1977. In 1966, there was only one instance in which this form of punishment was applied. In 1980, there were 22,958 criminal homicides and fewer than a handful of executions . . .

I realize that a very great number of factors are involved in this extremely complex question, and I do not suggest for a moment that the de facto end of the death penalty as a form of punishment is solely responsible for the burgeoning homicide rate in the United States. But I suggest it is equally unrealistic to assume that there is no relationship between the two.

The danger of resorting solely to statistics in attempting to determine the best course of action to follow in something as complex as the issue of the death penalty is illustrated by some of the statistics cited to support its abolition. Opponents of capital punishment point to the criminal homicide rates in states which have legally banned the death penalty and claim support for their beliefs in the fact that the statistics in these states are lower than in some in which capital punishment continues to be legally permissible. The questionable nature of such statistics becomes immediately apparent when we realize that capital punishment as a practical matter has all but ceased to exist in all states. When ten years pass without a single state exacting the death penalty, then statistics comparing states with capital punishment and those without become ridiculous.

Further, there is no evidence that shows that the death penalty is not a deterrent. Rational men fear death more than anything else. The use of the death penalty, therefore, has a potentially greater general deterrent effect than any other punishment.

Deterrence

A number of scholars have questioned the superior deterrent effectiveness of the death penalty. The most frequent form of attack is based on statistical arguments similar to the following:

1. There is no discernible statistical association between the existence of the death penalty and the willful homicide rate.
2. States that have abolished the death penalty have not shown a statistically significant increase in their willful homicide rates.
3. States that once abolished the death penalty and then

reintroduced it show no statistically significant decrease in their willful homicide rates.

4. Comparisons of contiguous states, one state with and the other without the death penalty, show no variation in the willful homicide rates that can be attributed to the existence of the death penalty.

Statistical arguments, like the above, however, are of limited value: they say only that the death penalty's general deterrence superiority compared with alternative punishments has not been demonstrated significantly. It has yet to be shown, however, that the death penalty is not more effective than other punishments. Failure to prove an effect does not mean there is no effect . . .

Conclusion

Gentlemen, I am of the belief that capital punishment must be assessed only after every legal safeguard has been provided and that it can be properly applied only with a full understanding of the great gravity of its exercise. But I am convinced and I urge you to conclude that capital punishment under carefully prescribed conditions as set forth in

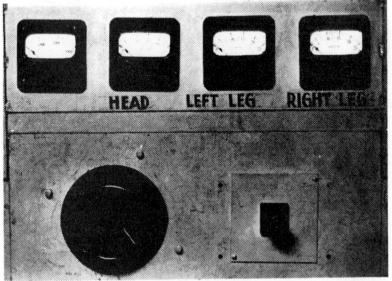

Tennessee Death-Control

Gregg v. Georgia and for highly selective offenses is a deterrent to certain kinds of crimes and that the value of human life is not lessened but is rather protected by retention of the death penalty as a form of punishment.

It is not the murderer alone that we are trying to reform with the death penalty: the true beneficiary of the criminal justice system is the law abiding populace. The more systematically we eliminate murderers by executions, the greater will be the reinforcement against killing and the greater the number of innocent lives saved. Compromising the protection of society, the true goal of the criminal justice system, to preserve the lives of a few criminals is a needless sacrifice of the innocent.

CAPITAL PUNISHMENT MEANS RACIAL BIAS

Massachusetts Labor Committee

The Massachusetts Labor Committee has formed a state-wide campaign against the restoration of the death penalty. The following statement asserts that minorities and poor people suffer from discrimination when the death penalty is used.

Points to Consider

1. What people participate in the decision to seek and carry out a death sentence?
2. What pattern is evident in the use of capital punishment?
3. What arguments are used to support the idea that capital punishment is an instrument of racism?
4. How did the Catholic Bishops sum up the matter of discrimination?

Excerpted from a position paper by the Massachusetts Campaign Against the Restoration of the Death Penalty, August, 1982.

From the founding of this country until today, capital punishment has been an instrument of racism.

Because our intuitive notions of fairness require that persons who break the same law under similar circumstances should meet with the same punishment, it is always disturbing to learn that American justice is inconsistent. In the case of capital crimes, such inconsistency is intolerable. It cannot be denied that most persons convicted of murder are not executed; only a few unlucky ones, (about one in five hundred) are killed by the state.

This is one important reason why the death penalty does not deter crime, but it is also a measure of its fundamental immorality. As the Massachusetts Supreme Judicial Court wrote in 1980, "While other forms of punishment may be arbitrary in some measure, the death penalty requires special scrutiny for constitutionality . . . (because it) 'differs from all other forms of criminal punishment, not in degree but in kind' " (quoting from the U.S. Supreme Court's 1972 decision *Furman v. Georgia*).

At each step in the process of apprehending and trying a defendant, discretion, and thus, arbitrariness, is inevitable. Even at the height of its use, a half century ago, the death penalty was received by only a relative handful of persons convicted of murder. At no time has there been any good rationale for the selection of those individuals. Where they happen to live is a prominent factor. Some counties seem to be "hanging counties" while others aren't. A study of plea-bargaining in Massachusetts murder cases revealed wide discrepancies from county to county in indictments, pleas, convictions, and sentences, differences that could *not* be explained solely by factors relevant to the crimes themselves.

Discrimination

There are many who now believe that discrimination in the use of death sentences against the poor and people of color has been eliminated by laws that require the jury to consider aggravating and mitigating circumstances prior to sentencing. This belief overlooks the fact that it is the prosecuting attorney who actually decides when and for whom to seek a death sentence. A judge and jury participate only after this initial decision has been made — a decision which has no regulatory standards to guide it.

In addition, a jury's decision of who is to die is based on a number of factors that do not admit of scientific proof or clearcut resolution. Did the defendant "premeditate" the murder? Was the defendant "sane"? Can the killing reasonably be construed as self-defense? Such problematic legal, factual, and psychological criteria determine when the death penalty will be employed. It is not unheard of for a defendant to be sentenced to die and then acquitted on retrial on the basis of exactly the same evidence. Is it reasonable that people's very lives should rest on such unstable factors?

Furthermore, some have argued that capital punishment is based not on requirements of justice at all but on a collective desire for a scapegoat. As a society we are not dealing effectively with the complex social problems that cause crime, so that executing an occasional criminal merely pretends to deal with this problem.

Searches in Vain

"One searches our chronicles in vain for the execution of any member of the affluent strata of our society."

Justice William Douglas, U.S. Supreme Court.

Pattern in the Use of the Death Penalty

Actually, the death penalty's administration reflects more than chance. There *is* a pattern to its use. Poor people and black people are singled out to be executed with disproportionate frequency. Clinton Duffy, San Quentin's former warden, put it succinctly: "The death penalty is a privilege of the poor." Those who can afford good, private lawyers invariably live, while those who are represented by overworked, under-experienced court-appointed lawyers often die. "One searches in vain for the execution of any member of the affluent strata of our society," said former Supreme Court Justice William O. Douglas (*Furman v. Georgia,* pp.251-252).

From the founding of this country until today, capital punishment has been an instrument of racism. Black people constitute about 12% of the population and 41% of the death row population. Study after study has substantiated the existence of racial discrimination and proven that race is, indeed, a key variable in sentencing.

- A Pennsylvania study found that fewer black people than white people had their sentences commuted, and race alone explained the disparity.

- Ninety percent of those executed for rape in the United States were black. Racism is added to racism when one realizes that the race of the *victim* also is a significant determinant of which criminal will be executed. No white man has ever been executed for raping a black woman.

- In Massachusetts, the only person every given the mandatory death sentence after conviction for felony-murder-rape was a black man whose victim was white.

- In Ohio between 1974 and 1977, there were 173 cases in which a black person killed a white person: 25% of the black people were sentenced to death. Out of 47 cases where a white killed a black, *none* of the whites was sentenced to death.

- Of 842 black people convicted of murdering white people in 1973 through 1977 in Florida, Texas, and Georgia, 126 were sentenced to die; of 294 white people convicted of murdering black people, 3 were sentenced to die.

In 1972, the U.S. Supreme Court held the death penalty unconstitutional because of facts like these. In 1976, it accepted some death penalty statutes provided they contained safeguards against arbitrariness and discrimination. Unfortunately, such changes were purely cosmetic and so served to mask the underlying unfairness of capital punishment. Arbitrariness and discrimination are *inherent* in a system of capital punishment, as the Massachusetts Supreme Judicial Court found in 1980. This is why former Supreme Court Justice Abe Fortas wrote, "All of the standards that can be devised to compel juries to impose the death penalty on capital offenders without exception or discrimination will be of no avail."

The Catholic Bishops of Massachusetts sum up the matter of discrimination quite well in their March 1982 statement, "It should be noted here also that we join other observers of the contemporary scene in acknowledging that the application of the death penalty is often unfair and discriminatory. A majority of those in prisons and on death row are poor, young and non-white. This means that those who have few financial resources or who are members of a racial or ethnic minority will be more likely to die, while those who are well off can avail themselves of the legal talent to present their cases in as convincing a light as possible."

COUNTERPOINT

RACIAL BIAS IS NO LONGER A VALID ARGUMENT

Lewis F. Powell, Jr.

The following statement was excerpted from an opinion by Supreme Court Justice Lewis F. Powell, Jr. in the case Furman v. Georgia. This 1972 decision held that death penalty statutes which leave the determination of whether the death penalty should be imposed to the unguided discretion of the jury or the court are unconstitutional.

Points to Consider

1. What social groups does capital punishment have the most impact on?
2. How does Justice Powell deal with this question?
3. What arguments are made that refute the thesis that capital punishment discriminates against minorities and the poor?
4. What is said about segregation in American society?

Excerpted from Furman v. Georgia, 408, U.S. 238 (1972).

The segregation of our society in decades past, which contributed substantially to the severity of punishment for interracial crimes, is now no longer prevalent in this country.

We are told that the penalty is imposed exclusively on uninfluential minorities — "the poor and powerless, personally ugly and socially unacceptable." Much is made of the undeniable fact that the death penalty has a greater impact on the lower economic strata of society, which includes a relatively higher percentage of persons of minority racial and ethnic group backgrounds . . .

As Mr. Justice Marshall's opinion today demonstrates, the argument does have a more troubling aspect. It is his contention that if the average citizen were aware of the disproportionate burden of capital punishment borne by the "poor, the ignorant, and the underprivileged," he would find the penalty "shocking to his conscience and sense of justice" and would not stand for its further use. This argument, like the apathy rationale, calls for further speculation on the part of the Court. It also illuminates the quicksands upon which we are asked to base this decision. Indeed, the two contentions seem to require contradictory assumptions regarding the public's moral attitude toward capital punishment. The apathy argument is predicated on the assumption that the penalty is used against the less influential elements of society, that the public is fully aware of this, and that it tolerates use of capital punishment only because of a callous indifference to the offenders who are sentenced. Mr. Justice Marshall's argument, on the other hand, rests on the contrary assumption that the public does not know against whom the penalty is enforced and that if the public were educated to this fact it would find the punishment intolerable . . .

Criminal Sanctions

Certainly the claim is justified that this criminal sanction falls more heavily on the relatively impoverished and under-

Pampering Murderers

Then, there's the argument that it's the blacks who are discriminated against. This one just doesn't wash! The record shows that over half those arrested for murder are black; but so are over half the victims! If black murderers are pampered, does this place a low value on black victims? We think not, and expect the black community will agree.

G. Russell Evans, *The American,* September, 1979.

privileged elements of society. The "have-nots" in every society always have been subject to greater pressure to commit crimes and to fewer constraints than their more affluent fellow citizens. This is, indeed, a tragic byproduct of social and economic deprivation, but it is not an argument of constitutional proportions under the Eighth or Fourteenth Amendment. The same discriminatory impact argument could be made with equal force and logic with respect to those sentenced to prison terms. The Due Process Clause admits of no distinction between the deprivation of "life" and the deprivation of "liberty." If discriminatory impact renders capital punishment cruel and unusual, it likewise renders invalid most of the prescribed penalties for crimes of violence. The root causes of the higher incidence of criminal penalties on "minorities and the poor" will not be cured by abolishing the system of penalties. Nor, indeed, could any society have a viable system of criminal justice if sanctions were abolished or ameliorated because most of those who commit crimes happen to be underprivileged. The basic problem results not from the penalties imposed for criminal conduct but from social and economic factors that have plagued humanity since the beginning of recorded history, frustrating all efforts to create in any country at any time the perfect society in which there are no "poor," no "minorities" and no "underprivileged."

The causes underlying this problem are unrelated to the constitutional issue before the Court.

Yet another theory for abolishing the death penalty — reflected in varying degrees in each of the concurring opinions today — is predicated on the discriminatory impact argument. Quite apart from measuring the public's acceptance or rejection of the death penalty under the "standards of decency" rationale, Mr. Justice Douglas finds the punishment cruel and unusual because it is "arbitrarily" invoked. He finds that "the basic theme of equal protection is implicit" in the Eighth Amendment, and that the Amendment is violated when jury sentencing may be characterized as arbitrary or discriminatory. While Mr. Justice Stewart does not purport to rely on notions of equal protection, he also rests

primarily on what he views to be a history of arbitrariness. Whatever may be the facts with respect to jury sentencing, this argument calls for a reconsideration of the "standards" aspects of the Court's decision in McGautha v. California. Although that is the unmistakable thrust of these opinions today, I see no reason to reassess the standards question considered so carefully in Mr. Justice Harlan's opinion for the Court last Term. Having so recently reaffirmed our historic dedication to entrusting the sentencing function to the jury's "untrammeled discretion", it is difficult to see how the Court can now hold the entire process constitutionally defective under the Eighth Amendment. For all of these reasons I find little merit in the various discrimination arguments, at least in the several lights in which they have been cast in these cases.

A Different Argument

Although not presented by any of the petitioners today, a different argument, premised on the Equal Protection Clause, might well be made. If a Negro defendant, for instance, could demonstrate that members of his race were being singled out for more severe punishment than others charged with the same offense, a constitutional violation might be established. This was the contention made in Maxwell v. Bishop, in which the Eighth Circuit was asked to issue a writ of habeas corpus setting aside a death sentence imposed on a Negro defendant convicted of rape. In that case substantial statistical evidence was introduced tending to show a pronounced disproportion in the number of Negroes receiving death sentences for rape in parts of Arkansas and elsewhere in the South. That evidence was not excluded but was found to be insufficient to show discrimination in sentencing in Maxwell's trial. Mr. Justice Blackmun, then sitting on the Eighth Circuit Court of Appeals, concluded:

"The petitioner's argument is an interesting one and we are not disposed to say it could not have some validity and weight in certain situations. Like the trial court, however . . . we feel that the argument does not have validity and pertinent application to Maxwell's case.

"We are not yet ready to condemn and upset the result reached in every case of a Negro rape defendant in the State of Arkansas on the basis of broad theories of social and statistical injustice . . .

"We do not say that there is no ground for suspicion that the death penalty for rape may have been discriminatorily applied over the decades in that large area of states whose statutes provide for it. There are recognizable indicators of this. But . . . improper state practice of the past does not automatically invalidate a procedure of the present . . .'"

I agree that discriminatory application of the death penalty in the past, admittedly indefensible, is no justification for holding today that capital punishment is invalid in all cases in which sentences were handed out to members of the class

80

discriminated against . . .

Conclusion

A final comment on the racial discrimination problem seems appropriate. The possibility of racial bias in the trial and sentencing process has diminished in recent years. The segregation of our society in decades past, which contributed substantially to the severity of punishment for interracial crimes, is now no longer prevalent in this country. Likewise, the day is past when juries do not represent the minority group elements of the community. The assurance of fair trials for all citizens is greater today than at any previous time in our history. Because standards of criminal justice have "evolved" in a manner favorable to the accused, discriminatory imposition of capital punishment is far less likely today than in the past.

A SOCIALIST CASE AGAINST CAPITAL PUNISHMENT

The People Newspaper

*The People **is the official publication of the Socialist Labor Party headquartered in Palo Alto, California. The following statement sets forth the socialist position on the death penalty. It argues the case of class bias and racism as the primary cause of crime and the death penalty as well.***

Points to Consider

1. How many people are on death row?
2. Why is capital punishment a weapon of class bias and racism?
3. Who are the real criminals and the real victims?
4. Why should the death penalty be abolished?

"The Socialist Case Against Capital Punishment," *The People,* February 4, 1984, pp. 6, 7.

It is not surprising that capital punishment fails to deter murder. Most crime is the result of the oppressive and dehumanizing social conditions that exist under capitalism.

Capitalism is guilty of so many crimes against workers that it is vain to try to determine which horror is the worst. But, certainly, the revival of the death penalty has to be one of the more damning indictments of inhuman brutality . . .

"The death penalty is barbaric and wrong," editorialized *The New York Times.* "It is state-sponsored killing that neither atones nor deters private murder."

Yet the death penalty is back. For almost 10 years, capitalism tried to get along without the death penalty. However, in its increasingly desperate efforts to preserve its dominant position in a rapidly disintegrating society, the capitalist class has renewed a weapon of class and racist terror — and can be expected to wield it with a vengeance.

There have been seven executions in the last 18 months — five in 1983 alone — compared with four in the first four years following the revival of executions in 1977. "We're now in the process of crossing the threshold from a point where executions are few and freakish to a point where they will become much more numerous and routine," Henry Schwarzschild, director of the American Civil Liberties Union's capital punishment project, said last year.

Currently, there are almost 1,300 inmates on death rows across the nation. Several dozen are in the final stages of appeals — their last hope of avoiding execution.

Those appeals are falling on increasingly deaf ears. After striking down then existing death-penalty laws in 1972, the U.S. Supreme Court upheld some revised state statutes in 1976. Since then, it has become more and more disposed to see capital sentences carried out.

The high court has even allowed some executions to be carried out without even bothering to review the constitutionality of the applicable state death-penalty laws. It has approved abbreviated appeal procedures and shown growing impatience with attorneys who raise questions of violation of due process and procedural safeguards. "Mere errors of state law are not the concern of this Court," declared Associate Justice William Rehnquist in regard to one case.

Specious Arguments

Proponents of the death penalty generally advance two arguments in their attempts to justify it: punishment and deterrence. Both arguments are specious.

"Murder must forfeit the murderer's life, if there is to be justice," argues the reactionary psychoanalyst Ernest van den Haag. This argument is simply an enunciation of the ancient brutal concept of the right of revenge, or the principle of an eye for an eye. It is what led Frederick Engels to note that "our capital punishment is nothing but blood revenge in a civilized form."

More than 125 years ago, Karl Marx gave short shrift to the then current versions of the punishment argument. "Plainly speaking, and dispensing with all paraphrases, punishment is nothing but a means of society to defend itself against the infraction of its vital conditions, whatever may be their character," Marx wrote. "Now, what a state of society is that, which knows of no better instrument for its own defense than the hangman, and which proclaims . . . its own brutality as eternal law?"

The second argument — deterrence — is more subtle but no more valid. It contends that executions deter murder. In a trivial sense, the argument is true: a person executed will kill no one in the future.

However, the main thrust of the deterrence argument is that executions serve to deter *others* from committing murder and other capital crimes. That argument rests on perverse reasoning and lacks factual support.

Marx, for example, noted: "It would be very difficult, if not altogether impossible, to establish any principle upon which the justice of capital punishment could be founded, in a society glorying in its civilization. Punishment in general has been defended as a means of intimidating. Now what right have you to punish me for the intimidation of others? And besides, there is history — there is such a thing as statistics — which prove with the most complete evidence that since Cain the world has neither been intimidated nor ameliorated by punishment."

There is still no evidence that supports the deterrence theory. As *The Christian Science Monitor* reported in July 1982, "no widely credited studies indicate the death penalty is a deterrent to murder, according to a variety of experts contacted by the Monitor."

A case in point is provided by the State of Florida. In the three years before the execution of John Spenkelink on May 25, 1979, Florida had an average of 904 homicides a year. In the three years following Spenkelink's well-publicized execution, the average number of homicides was 1,440. There is, moreover, some evidence that executions actually prompt an increase in homicides. Two researchers at the

---

Executing Children

However much the execution of children may seem like a relic of the past, the question is still with us. Only nine of the 39 states that use the death penalty recognize any age restrictions, and at least 30 prisoners on the death rows of 15 states were 17 or younger when their crimes were committed. Ten of these inmates — nine boys and one girl — were only 16. One, Joseph Aulisio in Pennsylvania, was 15.

David Bruck, *The Minneapolis Star and Tribune*, June 22, 1984.

Center of Applied Social Research at Northeastern University examined records of homicides and executions in New York State from 1907 to 1963. According to *The Christian Science Monitor,* "they found an average of two additional homicides in the month immediately following each execution, even when other variables were taken into account."

"The message of an execution is not deterrence," said one of the researchers. Instead, the message is "that lethal vengeance is the appropriate response to situations of feeling outraged and offended."

Roots of Crime

The death penalty does not deter violent crime. It cannot

reverse the damage done by crimes already committed. It can only add to the death toll and to the dehumanization of society in general.

It is not surprising that capital punishment fails to deter murder. Most crime is the result of the oppressive and dehumanizing social conditions that exist under capitalism. The effects of poverty, unemployment, festering slums, discrimination, broken homes, drug addiction and other social ills eventually push some individuals past the breaking point. They become what capitalist law calls criminals . . .

The social conditions responsible for most crime will remain as long as capitalism does. For they are the inevitable results of a system in which a small minority class owns and controls the means of production, robs the working class of the greater share of the wealth produced by its collective labor, and otherwise reaps the benefits of a system that condemns millions to lives of poverty and misery.

Given these facts, the death penalty can be viewed only as a means of repression used by the political state in an effort to shore up a deteriorating social order. Punishment and the threat of punishment are basic strategies in efforts to maintain order. And the death penalty is the supreme form of punishment.

Bill Andrews-*Daily World*

Former Texas Gov. John Connally says televised executions of prisoners "Would be an even more impressive deterrent" to crime

Class Bias and Racism

More than that, the death penalty is a weapon of class terror. Having no solution for the crime that capitalism breeds, the state selectively condemns to death working-class defendants who are, regardless of the crimes they may have committed, themselves victims of that evil system.

The nation's death rows are populated by the poor, the unemployed, the illiterate, members of oppressed minorities, drug addicts, alcoholics, and other outcasts. As the late Supreme Court Justice William O. Douglas once observed, "only those in the lower strata, only those who are members of an unpopular minority or the poor and despised" are executed.

More recently, Amnesty International confirmed the class bias of capital punishment. "Statistical surveys show that most of the condemned come from the ranks of the poor and unemployed," Amnesty reported.

These poor wretches come from the most oppressed segments of the working class. Subjected to the worst conditions that capitalism inflicts on workers, they are the most likely to commit those crimes which the state chooses to punish with death.

In addition, these poor working-class defendants are unable to afford the high-priced legal defenses that enable richer defendants to literally get away with murder. The poor are forced to rely on court-appointed counsel and public defenders who often lack resources, experience and expertise . . .

Abolish the Death Penalty

While more and more working-class victims of the capitalist system are condemned to death and executed, those who benefit from this unspeakably evil system kill workers with impugnity.

More than a hundred thousand workers are killed every year by industrial accidents and job-related diseases. Most of those deaths could be prevented . . .

It will take a social reorganization of society to get at the root of the oppressive social conditions and the steady degeneration of human relationships that are responsible for most of the murders, crime and antisocial behavior in this society. So too will it take a socialist reorganization of society to eliminate the crimes with which capitalism victimizes workers.

COUNTERPOINT

A CONSERVATIVE CASE
IN FAVOR OF
THE DEATH PENALTY

Walter Berns

Walter Berns is a resident scholar at the American Enter-
prise Institute for Public Policy Research. He is a prominent
national spokesman for conservative causes and principles,
and author of a book titled "For Capital Punishment—Crime
and the Morality of the Death Penalty".

Points to Consider

1. What does Dr. Berns say about the deterrence argument?
2. What argument does he make for capital punishment?
3. Why is the argument for the death penalty a modern one?
4. How is the author's argument different from the deterrence argument?

Excerpted from testimony by Walter Berns before the Committee on
the Judiciary of the United States Senate, 1981.

When 97.5 percent of the crimes committed in this country go unpunished, it would be foolish to expect to find that punishment of any sort deters. The fact is crime pays and criminals know it, and they act accordingly.

My argument in favor of capital punishment is not primarily a deterrence argument. The evidence on this question — that is to say, whether executions have a differential deterrence capacity or whether they, better than imprisonment, serve to deter potential murderers, for example — that evidence is disputed. You will be told that executions do not deter; that social science evidence demonstrates that executions do not deter, or do not deter any better than imprisonment; or that there is no evidence that they do.

You will also be referred to the sophisticated studies of Isaac Erlich which conclude that an execution may deter as many as eight murders. I, quite frankly, do not know who is right — Erlich or his many critics. My opinion, however, is — but I stress that it is only an opinion — that in our present situation when, as I calculate it, and I did this in the book, 97.5 percent of the crimes committed in this country go unpunished, it would be foolish to expect to find that punishment of any sort deters. The fact is crime pays and criminals know it, and they act accordingly.

Crime, of course, does not pay for some. They end up in prison. But, one suspects that those who end up in prison are the not-so-intelligent or the unlucky.

A Moral Argument

To repeat, the argument I make is not primarily a deterrence argument. It is a moral argument. In its general understanding it is also an old argument. One of the things I would like to say to this committee is that the proponents of capital punishment ought not to be deterred by the charges of immorality frequently made by the opponents of capital punishment.

As I have written, for example, no political philosopher with the qualified exception of Jeremy Bentham was opposed to capital punishment — not Aristotle; not Sir Thomas More; not Jean-Jacques Rousseau; not that great moralist Immanual Kant, not even John Stuart Mill, the great liberal.

The founders of the schools of human rights — for example John Locke — were not opposed to capital punishment; nor were the founders of this country — George Washington, Thomas Jefferson, et al.; nor was Abraham Lincoln.

The argument against punishment is a modern one. It coincides with a pervasive moral ambiguity. We punish these days with a bad conscience.

In my book I go into great detail with respect to two literary works, two literary masterpieces I think, dealing with murder and how murder should be punished. The first is Shakespeare's play "Macbeth," which Lincoln said was wonderful. The second is the modern novel by the Frenchman, Albert Camus, "The Stranger." Camus in fact was probably the most eloquent opponent of the death penalty. This novel does not deal with the death penalty as such, but the novel is related to it because the argument he makes in that novel is essentially that it is precisely a nonmoral society that may not execute or in fact that may not punish anyone for any crime.

Now I am not saying here or in the article that I have

Popular Support

The Harris survey in January, a few weeks after the lethal injection execution of a convicted slayer in Texas, found that 68 percent of those queried support capital punishment and 27 percent oppose it, with the remaining 5 percent "undecided." Twice as many were recorded in the undecided category a decade ago when death penalty proponents topped the opponents 59 percent to 31 percent.

George B. Merry, *The Christian Science Monitor*, May 11, 1983.

submitted to you or in the book that there is no moral case to be made against capital punishment. There surely is. It has traditionally been imposed in this country in a grossly discriminatory fashion. It remains to be seen whether this country can impose the death penalty without regard to race or class. If we cannot, if we impose it on poor blacks and send our rich white murderers to prison, the death penalty will have to be invalidated on equal protection grounds.

It is an extraordinary punishment and should be reserved for extraordinary criminals, and there are extraordinary criminals who are white — James Earl Ray being one; Richard Speck being another; Charles Manson being a third, none of whom was executed.

The Main Points

My moral argument briefly goes as follows. I will list a number of points here and go over them as briefly as I can:

One, we punish in part for retributive reasons, which is to say we want to pay the criminal back.

Two, this desire to pay back arises out of our anger and the moral indignation that accompanies that anger.

Three, anger, while of course it has to be tamed, has to be calmed — and that is, of course, one function of the law — anger is altogether proper. A society without anger or without citizens capable of being angry when their fellow citizens are the victims of criminals, is a society consisting entirely of Kitty Genovese's neighbors — and I assume the reference to Kitty Genovese is understood. She was the poor victim of a crime in Queens — I forget how many years ago, about 15 probably — who was mugged and eventually murdered. Many people heard her screaming in the night and no one came to her assistance and no one even bothered to call the police. As I say, a society consisting entirely of people like that, people like Kitty Genovese's neighbors, would be a society not worth living in. No one would care for anyone else. It would be a wholly selfish society.

Four, anger aroused by the sight of crime committed against others is a sign of caring for others. That anger is a sign of caring for others.

Five, in this respect it resembles love and is like love and is dissimilar to jealousy or greed, two human passions that

are I think wholly selfish. Anger, like love, is not wholly selfish.

Six, the law should respect such anger, In fact, the law as one of its functions should satisfy that anger.

Seven, the law satisfies that anger when it punishes the object of that anger, the criminal.

Eight, when it satisfies that anger it rewards it, it justifies it. The law says, in effect, to be angry in such circumstances is to demonstrate a sense of and a desire for justice.

Nine, by rewarding the anger the law promotes law-abidingness; it promotes good habits. It has what a Norwegian criminologist, Johannes Andenaes, calls a "general deterrent effect"; that is, it deters crime not by instilling fear, the fear of punishment, although as I say it may do that, but it deters by rewarding such anger. It inculcates law-abiding habits . . .

The Deterrence Argument

I would say that there is something useful about punishment and capital punishment.

My argument is not the ordinary deterrence argument, by which I meant of course deterrence as it is understood in criminology, which means we punish someone in order to inculcate fear in the hearts of others, and therefore, hope to prevent them from committing the crimes committed by the person we are punishing.

To repeat, that is something useful. If it were not useful, I suppose that no argument could be made for it. It is useful in a more subtle sense.

My argument is that it is useful to instill in citizens the sense of the awesomeness of the law precisely because the law is not simply an arbitrary statute that you and your colleagues here and in the House enact or an arbitrary statute that is enacted by a State legislature. We enact these statutes against murder, for example, precisely because it is morally wrong to murder, and we want people to understand that it is morally wrong to murder and to commit other crimes. There is nothing arbitrary about it.

How does one do that? How does one inculcate in the minds of people in the United States that it is wrong to do certain things? Well, we in this country, of course, have always relied on private institutions to do it. As I pointed out in my statement that I recited, this is a country which is forbidden by its principles from preaching. If there is going to be preaching, it is going to be done under the auspices of private institutions.

That leaves us, in a sense, with one public institution that we might use so as to inculcate certain good habits. I think that the criminal law is such an institution. It inculcates, as I say, by respecting this anger that you and I ought to feel, that good citizens ought to feel, when someone else is the victim of crime.

One has to argue here against Freud who argues that anger is simply a selfish passion. I do not believe that. I think it is entirely possible for a person to be angry. Rosie Grier was angry when the person he loved, Bobby Kennedy, was shot down in front of his eyes. There is no selfishness in that, it seems to me. That is a respectable passion. It has to be satisfied. When the law satisfies it by punishing Sirhan Sirhan and others, it therefore rewards that anger and, as I argue, inculcates the sense of right and wrong.

We have now reached the point in this country where when someone attempts to assassinate the President of the United States, immediately that provokes a good deal of sociological inquiry in the press. It turns out that this alleged assassin Hinckley was trying to score some points with a woman whom he admired from afar, a freshman at Yale University and a former movie actress.

We have it seriously discussed in the press that he is trying to make a political statement. The idea that one can make a political statement by taking the life of another human being is a horrible idea. One makes political statements by carrying placards.

Now we are asked to consider that the shooting of a President of the United States is rather like a man going before a radical feminist rally and dropping his trousers, a political statement of some sort. Well, it is not a political statement, and it is improper for the press even seriously to consider it as a political statement.

The law, I argue, must somehow inculcate that in our hearts and minds because the criminal law is the one institution we have in this country that allows us to work on the problem. The crime rate in this country indicates the degree of the problem.

EXECUTING INNOCENT PEOPLE

American Civil Liberties Union vs. Strom Thurmond

The American Civil Liberties Union is a non-profit political organization that claims to defend people who have had their basic rights violated. From a liberal perspective it opposes efforts by the Federal Government, State and local governments and private organizations that violate constitutional rights and liberties. Strom Thurmond is a conservative United States senator from South Carolina.

Points to Consider

1. How many innocent people have been executed?
2. What does Senator Thurmond say about executions of innocent people?
3. How does the public feel about capital punishment?
4. Which argument do you agree with? Why?

The following counterpoints were excerpted respectively from a position paper by the American Civil Liberties Union and a Senate report by Senator Strom Thurmond for the U.S. Senate Committee on the Judiciary, 1981.

The Point: American Civil Liberties Union

Pitts and Lee were sentenced to death in 1963 after local authorities beat a confession out of them. Their execution was delayed because the question of capital punishment was being heard in the U.S. Supreme Court.

Meanwhile, a white man confessed. The evidence pointed to his guilt. But Florida authorities weren't interested in the real murderer. "We already got two niggers for that," they said. It took years of legal battle, until 1975, before the governor's pardon came.

Twelve years and 28 days after the court had ordered them executed, Freddie Pitts and Wilbert Lee walked beyond the prison gates, each with $100 and a bus ticket in his pocket. Had the question of the death penalty not been before the courts — had their sentences been carried out on schedule — Pitts and Lee would have died innocent men.

What if they had been executed? Would anyone have come forth with new evidence? Would anyone have spent years to prove their innocence? What difference would a confession have made? For how many innocent people has the truth come too late?

Our criminal justice system is supposed to insure against such injustice.

Yet just four months after Pitts and Lee were released, history repeated itself. Newspaper headlines read BIKERS CLEARED OF MURDER. Four innocent men had spent 18 months on death row in New Mexico, convicted of a gory mutilation slaying that had tempers running hot. The four, members of a motorcycle gang that had passed through town, were an unsympathetic lot. They made an easy target for local authorities. Despite a weak case, the prosecutor had no trouble getting a conviction.

The execution was delayed as the Supreme Court once again heard a death penalty case. While the four waited on death row, another man confessed. He even drew a map of the murder site. A reluctant district attorney was forced to release the men he had sought to have put to death.

These are examples of the hundreds of documented cases where victims of injustice managed to stay alive long enough to be exonerated. But others have not been blessed with such good timing.

Death is a punishment absolute. Final. There are no more appeals. No reversals. It is an irrevocable punishment carried out by a criminal justice system that is far from perfect. And can never be perfect, as long as it is run by human beings. Because human beings make mistakes.

There are many reasons the death penalty is wrong. It doesn't serve as a deterrent. It doesn't lower the homicide rate. It doesn't protect society. It certainly doesn't rehabilitate. It is used against the poor, the uneducated, against blacks and other minorities. It may even encourage the taking of life by its own poor example.

Marquis de Lafayette wrote, "I shall ask for the abolition of the punishment of death until I have the infallibility of human judgment presented to me."

The Counterpoint: Senator Strom Thurmond

It is the conclusion of this committee that it is not enough to proclaim the sanctity and importance of innocent life. Innocent life must be, and can only be, secured by a society that is willing to impose its highest penalty upon those who threaten such life. As observed by Professor Walter Berns:

> We think that some criminals must be made to pay for their crimes with their lives, and we think that we, the survivors of the world they violated, may legitimately extract that payment because we, too, are their victims. By punishing them, we demonstrate that there are laws that bind men across generations as well as across (and within) nations, that we are not simply isolated individuals, each pursuing his selfish interests.

Possibility of Error

An argument that is often asserted in favor of abolition of capital punishment concerns the dangers of executing the innocent. It is pointed out that if such an error occurs, it is irremediable. The argument is then made that, since the cost of such a mistake is so great, the risk of permitting the death penalty to be imposed at all is unacceptable.

The Committee finds this argument to be without great weight, particularly in light of the procedural safeguards for criminal defendants mandated by the Supreme Court in recent years. The Court's decision with respect to the rights of the individual, particularly those expending the right to counsel, together with the precautions taken by any court in a capital case, have all reduced the danger of error in these cases to that of a mere theoretical possibility. Indeed, the Committee is aware of no case where an innocent man has been put to death. Admittedly, however, due to the fallible nature of man, this possibility does continue to exist. Insofar as it does, it is the opinion of the Committee that this minimal risk is justified by the protection afforded to society by the death penalty. As stated in the minority report of the Massachusetts Special Commission:

> We do not feel, however, that the mere possibility of error, which can never be completely ruled out, can be urged as a reason why the right of the state to inflict the death penalty can be questioned in principle. All that can be expected of [human authorities] is that they take every reasonable precaution against the danger of error. When this is done by those who are charged with the application of the law, the likelihood that errors will be made descends to an irreducible minimum. If errors are then made, this is the necessary price that must be paid within a society which is made up of human beings and whose authority is exercised not by angels but by men themselves. It is not brutal or unfeeling to suggest that the danger of miscarriage of justice must be weighed against the far greater evils for which the death penalty aims to provide effective remedies.

Public Opinion

In arriving at a decision to support the death penalty, considerable weight was given to public opinion on the acceptability of the death penalty. Contrary to the frequently asserted statement that there is growing public opposition to capital punishment, examination of public opinion polls over the last ten years shows a remarkable rise in the number of Americans in favor of the death penalty. A Gallup opinion poll revealed that public support for the death penalty for murder has reached its highest point in 28 years — and this poll was taken before the attempt on the President's life. Sixty-six percent — two in every three Americans — favor the death penalty for persons convicted of murder. In 1971, forty-nine percent of the public approved of capital punishment for murder. It appears from the polls, and from a flood of recent correspondence that a demand for the death penalty coincides with a greater public awareness of the crime problem.

WHAT IS EDITORIAL BIAS?

This activity may be used as an individualized study guide for students in libraries and resource centers or as a discussion catalyst in small group and classroom discussions.

The capacity to recognize an author's point of view is an essential reading skill. The skill to read with insight and understanding involves the ability to detect different kinds of opinions or bias. Sex bias, race bias, ethnocentric bias, political bias and religious bias are five basic kinds of opinions expressed in editorials and all literature that attempts to persuade. They are briefly defined in the glossary below.

5 Kinds of Editorial Opinion or Bias

*sex bias — the expression of dislike for and/or feeling of superiority over the opposite sex or a particular sexual minority

*race bias — the expression of dislike for and/or feeling of superiority over a racial group

*ethnocentric bias — the expression of a belief that one's own group, race, religion, culture or nation is superior. Ethnocentric persons judge others by their own standards and values.

*political bias — the expression of political opinions and attitudes about domestic or foreign affairs

*religious bias — the expression of a religious belief or attitude.

Guidelines

1. From the readings in chapter three, locate five sentences that provide examples of editorial opinion or bias.

2. Write down each of the above sentences and determine what kind of bias each sentence represents. Is it sex bias,

race bias, ethnocentric bias, political bias or religious bias?

3. Make up one sentence statements that would be an example of each of the following: sex bias, race bias, ethnocentric bias, political bias and religious bias.

4. See if you can locate five sentences that are factual statements from the readings in chapter three.

5. What is the editorial message of the cartoon on page 86?

CHAPTER 4

CAPITAL PUNISHMENT IN FOREIGN COUNTRIES

THE NEED FOR WORLDWIDE ABOLITION

Amnesty International

Amnesty International acts on the behalf of the U.N. Universal Declaration of Human Rights and other international instruments. Through practical work for prisoners within its mandate, AI participates in the wider promotion and protection of human rights in the civil, political, economic, social and cultural spheres. Each year it conducts a major worldwide campaign against the use of torture.

Points to Consider

1. What justifications are used by governments that kill their citizens?
2. What progress is being made toward worldwide abolition of capital punishment?
3. How is the death penalty used in China?
4. What does the International Declaration of Stockholm say about the death penalty?

Excerpted from *Amnesty Action,* 1984, and a position paper by Amnesty International U.S.A. in 1983.

Amnesty International opposes the death penalty unconditionally because it violates the right to life and the right to be free from cruel, inhuman and degrading treatment or punishment as guaranteed in the Universal Declaration of Human Rights.

Despite a United Nations resolution calling for the restriction and eventual abolition of the death penalty, there are 128 countries with death penalty laws in force. In the past five years, 55 of them have used that authority to execute thousands.

Almost every government that kills its citizens offers the justification of a 'higher social objective.' Only the objective itself changes: preventing revolution (Iraq) . . . protecting revolution (Ethiopia) . . . immorality (Iran) . . . murder (U.S.A.) . . . armed robbery (Nigeria) . . . drug trafficking (Singapore) . . . economic crimes (U.S.S.R.) . . . stopping terrorism (South Africa) . . .

The American who recoils in horror at the execution of adulterers in Iran or the torture of alleged revolutionaries in Argentina, while demanding death for murderers in the U.S., is not reflecting different values so much as responding to a different threat. The threat may be violence stemming from social disintegration, rather than violence stemming from political instability. But the solution chosen by those in power in both situations is to inflict pain and/or death on selected human beings.

In the decade from 1969-1979:
- more than 7500 people were sentenced to die worldwide
- more than 5000 were executed
- more than 500,000 were victims of political killings.

In the calendar year 1980:
- there were 1229 known executions
- more than 1000 executions were carried out by 8 countries

The United Nations has found that "it is generally agreed between the retentionists and the abolitionists, whatever their opinions about the validity of comparative studies of deterrence, that the data which now exist show no correlation between the existence of capital punishment and lower rates of capital crime." According to INTERPOL (International Criminal Police) statistics, most countries which have abolished the death penalty have lower rates of murder and attempted murder. A recent study of the use of the death penalty in New York State between 1907 and 1963 shows that there were, on the average, two additional homicides in the month following an execution.

On a worldwide basis, the death penalty is overwhelmingly imposed on members of opposition groups, racial, religious and ethnic minorities. The almost exclusive imposition of the death penalty on the least powerful and/or most despised helps to explain the relative lack of outcry over its use in the U.S.

Abolition

Progress, however, is being made towards the worldwide abolition of the death penalty. In the spring of 1981, the Council of Europe passed a resolution calling for abolition of the death penalty among its member states. In 1979-80, Peru, Brazil and Nicaragua abolished the death penalty, either completely or for peacetime offenses. Canada abolished the death penalty in 1976 and France abolished it in September 1981.

Amnesty International opposes the death penalty unconditionally because it violates the right to life and the right to be free from cruel, inhuman and degrading treatment or punishment as guaranteed in the Universal Declaration of Human Rights. AI is seeking to foster the growing trend among many nations to eliminate the death penalty. It works to expose the alarming number of executions in countries such as Iran, South Africa and Pakistan, and to expose the continued widespread use of the death penalty in nations such as the U.S.S.R., Iraq and China. To this list must be added the U.S., which, with 924 men and women awaiting death as of December 1981, could become a world leader in legal killings.

AMNESTY
INTERNATIONAL

Recipient of 1977 Nobel Peace Prize

Death is Punishment for 29 Crimes in China

The recent wave of executions in China continues to evoke criticism from the international human rights community. Capital offenses in China now include theft, spying, organizing secret societies, corruption, embezzlement, and gang fighting.

Amnesty International documented 600 executions last fall, stressing that the total number is certainly greater. Foreign analysts estimate that 5,000 Chinese citizens may have been killed.

In a letter sent to President Li Xiannian last October, Amnesty called for a halt to use of the death penalty. China now imposes the death penalty for 29 crimes at a rate by far the highest since the early 1970s. Authorities have executed people in groups of 15 to 40, after parading them before mass rallies or through city streets.

Noting that the current executions are said to be part of a nationwide campaign against crime, Amnesty said that the death penalty had never been shown to be a more effective deterrent than other punishments. Moreover, Amnesty wrote, "Once an innocent person is executed, the error can never be corrected."

The majority of those executed appear to be unemployed people aged between 18 and 40. The time limit for appeal after sentencing has been reduced to three days.

In its response to Amnesty, China's Foreign Ministry said, "Criminals should be given punishment that they deserve in accordance with the law. This is a normal measure and routine work to maintain the public security of a country."

Amnesty International Conference on the Abolition of the Death Penalty
Declaration of Stockholm, 11 December 1977

The Stockholm Conference on the Abolition of the Death Penalty, composed of more than 200 delegates and participants from Africa, Asia, Europe, the Middle East, North and South America and the Caribbean region, RECALLS THAT:
• The death penalty is the ultimate cruel, inhuman and degrading punishment and violates the right to life.

CONSIDERS THAT:

- The death penalty is frequently used as an instrument of repression against opposition, racial, ethnic, religious and underprivileged groups,
- Execution is an act of violence, and violence tends to provoke violence,
- The imposition and infliction of the death penalty is brutalizing to all who are involved in the process,
- The death penalty has never been shown to have a special deterrent effect,
- The death penalty is increasingly taking the form of unexplained disappearances, extra-judicial executions and political murders,
- Execution is irrevocable and can be inflicted on the innocent,

AFFIRMS THAT:

- It is the duty of the state to protect the life of all persons within its jurisdiction without exception,
- Executions for the purposes of political coercion, whether by government agencies or others, are equally unacceptable,
- Abolition of the death penalty is imperative for the achievement of declared international standards,

DECLARES:

- Its total and unconditional opposition to the death penalty,
- Its condemnation of all executions, in whatever form, committed or condoned by governments,
- Its commitment to work for the universal abolition of the death penalty,

CALLS UPON:

- Non-governmental organizations, both national and international, to work collectively and individually to provide public information materials directed towards the abolition of the death penalty,
- All governments to bring about the immediate and total abolition of the death penalty,
- The United Nations unambiguously to declare that the death penalty is contrary to international law.

16 READING GLOBAL PERSPECTIVES

THE DETERRENT EFFECT OF EXECUTIONS IN JAPAN

The Japanese Government

The following statement is excerpted from a position paper by the Japanese Government on the use of capital punishment in Japan. It deals with the deterrent effect of the death penalty. It also offers information about the social motives for executions and how extensively they are applied in Japanese law.

Points to Consider

1. Why is capital punishment considered a deterrent in Japan?
2. How extensive is the application of the death penalty?
3. Under what circumstances is capital punishment used?
4. How popular is the death penalty in Japan?

Excerpted from a Japanese Government position paper issued to the publisher in 1984 by the Japanese Embassy in Washington, D.C.

Capital punishment in Japan is imposed infrequently and then only after completion of impeccable judicial and administrative procedures. There is widespread popular acceptance of it.

Retention or abolition of the death penalty is an issue inappropriate to resolution at the international level, simply because it is too closely related, not to crime rates and criminal justice administration alone, but to each nation's history, culture, and ethical and moral norms. Japan, to illustrate, retains the death penalty at the same time that it manifests decreasing crime rates, a low frequency of serious offenses and a stable social and political order. It is widely accepted among Japanese citizens that the safe, secure environment in which they live is very much a product of the deterrent effect wrought by the retention of capital punishment, and not only by an effective implementation of national political and economic policies for social justice and an efficient and fair administration of criminal justice.

Law Enforcement

Japanese law enforcement officers are instructed and trained to refrain as far as possible from using lethal forces even when confronted by the use of firearms by dangerous offenders; they try to reduce such criminals to control without inflicting even the slightest injuries. For example, in 1972, five members of the Japan Red Army, a radical terrorist organization, who were personally responsible for deaths of and injuries to many persons, entrenched themselves in a mountain cabin with a hostage and discharged volleys of firearms at the police surrounding them. They were finally taken into custody without any wounds despite the fact that during their resistance they killed three police officers and seriously wounded 15 or 16 others. Such admirable restraint on the part of Japanese law enforcement authorities is motivated by a belief that in the long run such a policy encourages even serious offenders to submit peacefully to arrest and to allow the justice of their claims to be adjudicated by the courts. But restraint of such a commendable order is possible only if capital punishment is available against those who willfully kill. The broad base of public support for the death penalty is demonstrated through responses to public opinion surveys.

Nevertheless, the extreme sanction is quite sparingly used in Japan. It governs only 17 offenses, ten of which comprehend conduct directly dangerous to human life (e.g., intentional homicide, trainwrecking causing death), three of which embody collective action jeopardizing public safety (e.g., leading an insurrection), and four of which pose substantial danger to a community (e.g., arson of inhabited structures). Moreover, life imprisonment or imprisonment with or without labor for a term of years is an available alternative sanction for every crime except inducement of foreign aggression.

Despite general public acceptance of capital punishment in Japan, the matter of retention and scope of the death penalty in Japanese penal legislation has been under active review for several years in the context of a project to prepare a revised Penal Code. The Legislative Council of the Ministry of Justice, an advisory organ to the Minister of Justice, evaluated many aspects of the issue, including the moral responsibility of criminals who committed the gravest offenses, the value of respect for human life, attitudes of victims or survivors, general educative impact and deterrent effect of capital punishment, and its impact on trial procedures, and made a comparative study of legal provisions governing and actual frequency of use of the death penalty in other nations. Although not without vigorous dissent, the Council concluded that abolition of capital punishment is not desirable at this stage of Japanese history; heinous crimes still occur and a majority of the public strongly endorses the death penalty. However, in a 1974 report to the Minister of Justice, the Council did recommend that the scope of the penalty be reduced by eliminating it as a sanction for six offenses in the present Penal Code, and that the alternative of life imprisonment should be introduced for the offense of inducement of armed foreign aggression. The Council also proposed to introduce a special provision requesting the court to use utmost care in imposing the death penalty. Such changes are likely to be accepted by the Diet when it acts on the draft Penal Code in the near future.

A Narrow Focus

Japanese law forbids capital punishment of offenders under 18 years of age at the time of commission of their offenses; punishment must be reduced to life imprisonment (Juvenile Law art. 51). In addition, the Minister of Justice is required to enter an order of stay of execution if a person sentenced to death is legally to be characterized as insane or if a woman so sentenced is pregnant.

Japanese sentencing courts are most sparing in assessing the death penalty. They carefully assess the factors crucial to capital sentencing, including the offender's age, personality, life history and personal circumstances; the motivation for, method of commission of, and results of the offense; the impact of the crime on the community and community attitudes; the offender's personal attitude after commission of the crime; and consonance of a death sentence in the particular case with dispositions in a long accumulation of capital and noncapital cases reviewed by appellate courts. It is impossible to assert that the death penalty is invoked capriciously by Japanese courts.

There has been steady decline in the frequency with which capital punishment has been invoked and carried out; the only exception to the trend was observable during a brief period following the close of the Pacific War, to be explained by the turbulent social conditions prevailing at the time. Thus, from 1974 through 1978, only 13 persons, or an average of 2.6 persons each year, were sentenced to death, and the penalty in fact was invoked only against persons who had committed intentional homicide or inflicted death during commission of a robbery. Moreover, the circumstances under which those crimes were committed which resulted in exaction of the death penalty were so revolting that even opponents of capital punishment might hesitate to accept an alternative form of punishment: they involved multiple victims, careful planning or callous cruelty to children in the course of robbery or kidnapping.

To recapitulate, capital cases are most carefully evaluated and reviewed by three levels of courts, and all tribunals are composed of a minimum of three professionally-trained judges. After all judicial processes have been exhausted, the Minister of Justice, whose responsibility it is to enforce a sentence of death, sees that an intensive review is made of judicial records and relevant occurrences after completion of judicial action, to determine whether there exist grounds for new trial or amnesty. Only after such an administrative evaluation has taken place will the death penalty be carried through. If a new trial is requested by the convicted offender, the death sentence is stayed until the court decides on the propriety of opening a new trial.

In sum, capital punishment in Japan is imposed infrequently and then only after completion of impeccable judicial and administrative procedures. There is widespread popular acceptance of it. Nevertheless, the question of retention or abolition is sure to be a perennial subject for debate, domestically and internationally.

CAPITAL PUNISHMENT IN
THE SOVIET UNION

Ger P. van den Berg

Ger P. van den Berg is a British scholar who wrote the
following statement in the publication Soviet Studies, *a*
quarterly journal on the USSR and Eastern Europe published
by the University of Glasgow. His article deals with the
nature, motives and scope of capital punishment in the
Soviet Union.

Points to Consider

1. What problems do scholars have in researching the application of capital punishment in the USSR?
2. How extensive is the use of capital punishment in the Soviet Union?
3. What crimes may lead to the death penalty?
4. Why is the death penalty used?

Ger P. van den Berg, "The Soviet Union and the Death Penalty,"
Soviet Studies, April 2, 1983, pp.154-74.

On the basis of experience in other countries one could argue that the existence of the death penalty does not deter crime, since it is usually applied only in certain instances. The Soviet experience also suggests that a high frequency of application of the death penalty does not deter crime either.

In recent years, Western scholars have paid considerable attention to the existence of the death penalty in the Soviet Union. Soviet lawyers have also shown an interest in the reasons behind the continued existence of the death penalty in their country. These lawyers are, in general, critical of certain aspects of the death penalty, although they defend its application for some crimes and especially for murder under aggravating circumstances.

A major problem in trying to evaluate the reasons for the continued existence of the death penalty is the absence of figures regarding its application. Those figures mentioned in the West are mainly derived by counting the number of Soviet press reports on the carrying out of death sentences. The number of cases reported is about 30 each year. However, a recent Soviet emigré lawyer, Konstantin Simis, has estimated the actual number of death sentences at somewhere between 2,500 and 3,000 annually. His estimate is based on evidence put forward by the dissident Aleksander Ginzburg and on his own experience as a lawyer in the Soviet Union.

The question of the death penalty has to be considered in close relation to the question of terror, that is, the security police's power of summary execution. These questions are partly interrelated in Soviet law, since this power of the security police has been formalized, and indeed also has existed at times during which the security situation did not call for the formalization of power. Moreover, summary execution also has been used to deal with ordinary crimes . . .

Death Penalty in Peacetime

At the time of writing, the death penalty *in peacetime* is possible — although always optional — for the following offenses:

(a) political crimes
- treason (Article 64);
- espionage (Article 65);
- terrorist acts, if a public official (Article 66) or a representative of a foreign state (Article 67) is killed;
- sabotage (Article 68);
- organizational activities directed to commit one of the crimes listed *supra* (Article 72)'
- the commission of one of the above-listed crimes directed against another working people's state (Article 73);
- banditry (Article 73);
- action disrupting the work of prison camps (Article 77-1, introduced in 1962);

(b) economic crimes
- counterfeiting of money or securities as a form of business (Article 87; introduced in 1962);
- speculation in currency, speculation as a form of business or on a large scale or by a recidivist (Article 88; introduced in 1962);
- stealing of state property on an especially large scale (Article 93-1); introduced in 1962);
- taking of bribes by an official under certain circumstances (Article 173; introduced in 1962);

(c) crimes against the person
- intentional homicide under aggravating circumstances (Article 102;
- rape under certain circumstances (Article 117; introduced in 1962, mitigated in 1980);
- infringing the life of a policeman or people's guard (Article 191-2; introduced in 1962);
- hijacking of aircraft with grave consequences (Article 213-2; introduced in 1973);

(d) military crimes
- resisting of a superior by persons subject to military service, in conjunction with intentional homicide (Article 240).

Published laws and other sources are silent on the subject of the security police's right of summary execution. The decrees of 1922, 1923 and 1933 which provided the security police with the power of summary execution, were officially repealed in 1959, with the enactment of the new criminal procedural legislation.

Death by Shooting

The death penalty is carried out in the USSR by shooting. A death sentence may be passed only by a court, and only on conviction for a crime liable to punishment by death. Civilians charged with such offenses (or any other) are tried in the country's civil courts. Cases of espionage are the single exception: they are heard by military tribunals . . .

In the USSR, the death penalty may be imposed for 18 different offenses in peacetime, among them offenses not involving the use of violence.

Amnesty International Report, *The Death Penalty,* **1979.**

Number of Death Sentences in the Post Stalin Period

Figures on the application of the death penalty are not regularly published in the Soviet Union. The only available data are from 1966. The Belorussion criminologist Ella Sarkisova asserted in 1969:

> The application of the death penalty in the practice of the judicial agencies is extremely insignificant in comparison with other penalties. For example, in 1966 only 0.4% of convicted persons were sentenced to death by the Belorussian courts. The death penalty is applied mainly for intentional homicide and rape committed under aggravating circumstances by criminals, already previously sentenced by agencies of jusice, who did not show any signs of rehabilitation even after the application of strict criminal law measures.

Such a figure, if taken as being representative for the en-

tire USSR, would yield (0.004 x 650,000 =) 2,600 death
sentences in 1966 . . .

After Khrushchev

After Khrushchev's demise in the autumn of 1964, an attempt was made to restrict the application of the death
penalty. A 1965 study — commissioned by the Presidium of
the USSR Supreme Soviet and made by the USSR Institute
for the Study and Prevention of Crime on the application and
effectiveness of the death penalty in the years 1961-65 —
contained a proposal to abolish the death penalty at least
for economic crimes.

Apparently the proposals were rejected, but in 1971 the
Chairman of the USSR Supreme Court, A.F. Gorkin, urged
that they be reconsidered. The only immediate result was
that procedural rules were changed somewhat in 1970 in
cases in which the death penalty is possible.

At the same time, some jurists began to urge restrictions
on its application, especially for economic crimes. Moreover,
the communique of the World Congress of Peace-Loving
Forces (Moscow, October 1973) contained an appeal to do
away with the death penalty:

> Every individual has the inalienable right to life, which
> must be protected by law. The states have to aspire to the
> complete abolition of the death penalty. The right to life is
> connected with the question of the right to refuse to take
> the life of another.

In 1976 a book by Pavel Osipov concerning the theoretical
foundations of the system and application of criminal sanctions was published by the University of Leningrad. This
study contains the only elaborate plea for the abolition of
the death penalty published in recent years in the Soviet
Union . . .

This plea for a programme to abolish the death penalty is
the only one of its kind observed in Soviet literature. It is interesting to note that the arguments put forward by Osipov
do not differ in essence from those put forward by Andrei
Sakharov in his letter of 1977 to the Organising Committee
of the Conference on the Abolition of the Death Penalty,

convened by Amnesty International . . .

Osipov's book has been favorably reviewed in the Leningrad University Law Review *Pravovedenie* by N.A. Struchkov, the authority in the field of the law of execution of penalties, and others . . .

According to an opinion poll, carried out by Sarkisova, regarding the attitude of people towards the humaneness of Soviet criminal law, more than 90% of the interviewed persons declared that Soviet criminal laws are humane but

62% of them held the humaness of the laws as one of the causes for the commission of crimes. Many proposals were made by citizens on the need to perfect criminal legislation and to make it more severe. Some people also propose the introduction of the death penalty for minors who commit especially serious crimes.

According to the results of an opinion poll conducted recently among 10,000 employees in a number of factories in

Tashkent, 89.6% wanted to keep the death penalty. Out of a group of procurators, investigators, and judges, 90% were of the same opinion, although an absolute majority of advocates (lawyers) favored its abolition. The jurist B.A. Mirensky, who lectures at the Tashkent Police College, concludes that conditions for the abolition of the death penalty do not yet exist; ' . . . as long as crimes such as banditry, intentional homicide under aggravating circumstances and some others occur, it is necessary to resort to the death penalty, this temporary and exceptional measure of punishment'.

Sarkisova finds decisive arguments for maintaining the death penalty in its retributive effect in cases of first-degree murder:

> The possibility of applying the supreme measure of punishment for this crime is in harmony with the principles of socialist humanism and the task of optimally protecting human life. Those who are capable of taking the life of others should pay with their own life.

Therefore, she agrees with proposals to abolish the death penalty for theft of state property and also argues for its abolition in cases of bribery..

It seems evident from the arguments put forward by Osipov and Sarkisova that the central question is the abolition of the death penalty for those capital crimes which result in the loss of life.

Conclusion

The continued existence of the death penalty and the frequency of its application in cases of first-degree murder can be seen as evidence of the influence of public opinion upon Soviet legal practice. The popular belief, echoed by some scholars, is that serious violent crimes may and shall not exist in a socialist society.

> One has to bear in mind that the serious crimes for which the culprits are sentenced to death are something monstrous, foreign to the socialist system and that the death penalty rightly serves as the means with the aid of which we will liquidate especially serious crimes in the shortest possible period.

On the basis of experience in other countries one could argue that the existence of the death penalty does not deter crime, since it is usually applied only in certain instances. The Soviet experience also suggests that a high frequency of application of the death penalty does not deter crime either.

It is impossible to predict the future of the death penalty in the Soviet Union. One could perhaps expect abolition of the death penalty for economic crimes. Moreover, the number of death sentences for war criminals will decrease for obvious reasons. But, public opinion on the one hand, and the opinion prevailing among the political leadership on the other hand that criminality is a phenomenon foreign to socialism, will be forceful champions of maintaining the death penalty for certain violent crimes, and especially for first-degree murder. This notwithstanding the fact that Marxism-Leninism has a negative attitude to the death penalty, that the death penalty has only been 'provisionally' introduced, and that an abolitionist programme has been launched.

18 READING GLOBAL PERSPECTIVES

POLITICAL EXECUTIONS
IN IRAN

Amnesty International

*Amnesty International is a worldwide movement which is
independent of any government, political faction, ideology,
economic interest, or religious creed. It plays a specific role
within the overall spectrum of human rights work. The
activities of the organization focus strictly on prisoners:*

*• It seeks the release of men and women detained
anywhere for their beliefs, color, sex, ethnic origin, language,
or religion, provided they have neither used nor advocated
violence. These are termed "Prisoners of Conscience."*

*• It advocates fair and early trials for all political prisoners
and works on behalf of such persons detained without
charge or without trial.*

*• It opposes the death penalty and torture or other cruel,
inhuman or degrading treatment or punishment of all
prisoners without reservations.*

Points to Consider

1. What happened after the revolution in Iran?
2. What people were being executed?
3. Why were executions taking place?
4. What do reports say about executing children?

Excerpted from Amnesty International Documentation on Iran, 1982.

123

There have been many reports of the execution of children and pregnant women.

Since the revolution of February 1979 Amnesty International's concerns in Iran have been executions, cruel, inhuman and degrading treatment of prisoners, lack of fair trials and the detention of prisoners of conscience (persons imprisoned because of their political or religious beliefs or by reason of their ethnic origin, sex, color or language, who have not used or advocated violence). Amnesty International has maintained a record of the number of executions which have been announced by the Iranian authorities and reported outside Iran. It has also published a report, *Law and Human Rights in the Islamic Republic of Iran,* which criticizes the procedures of the Islamic Revolutionary Courts. Although Amnesty International has from time to time published information about the ill-treatment of prisoners and about prisoners of conscience, it has been extremely difficult to document these concerns because of the fears of prisoners and their families that publicity or any other form of drawing attention to the treatment of individual prisoners might be harmful to them or bring about the arrest of relatives. These fears are shared by Iranians who have been able to leave the country illegally, but have relatives still in Iran. For this reason Amnesty International has been able to refer to individual cases only when relatives have decided to accept the risks involved in publicity, or when the prisoner was dead.

Identifying prisoners of conscience amongst the thousands of people arrested for political reasons in Iran since the revolution has been very difficult because of the impediments which prevent investigation of individual cases, because of the imprecision of the charges, even when these are known, and because of the lack of fair trials which in most cases prevent Amnesty International from assessing with any accuracy the validity of the charges.

In most cases known to Amnesty International people sentenced to death have been executed almost immediately after the passing of sentence, thus allowing no time for appeal.

Torture in Evin Prison

Most of those in Block Four are hit repeatedly across the testicle area. Old inmates in Block Four say that they estimate three out of ten men repeatedly beaten in this manner have died.

Evin officials recently ruled that men and women over 40 years old could be lashed only on their feet. The feet of these prisoners are twisted between strings before the soles are lashed. According to former inmates, the victim's legs "swell up like watermelons."

The notorious women's prison at Evin holds about 40 children between the ages of one and 12, along with their mothers. Children are forced to watch while guards whip their mothers. Guards are also said to strike the children and to threaten them with torture.

Matchbox, February, 1983.

Executions

In many cases executions appear to have taken place without any trial at all, but even in those cases where trials have occurred they appear to have been summary. Amnesty International was told of an instance of this which occurred in Iranian Kurdistan very shortly after the revolution in March 1979. The informant was one of 180 defendants in a trial which took place in a barn. The presiding judge was Ayatollah Khalkhali and at the end of the trial which lasted 2½ hours he sentenced 27 of the 180 defendants to death. They were executed very shortly afterwards . . .

Repeatedly Amnesty International has been told of relatives only learning of executions some time after they have taken place and of having been unable to find out whether or not the execution was preceded by a trial.

One informant spoke about the execution of his wife, whom he described as a sympathizer with the Mujahideen. He learned of her execution when it was announced on television and reported to the press, two days after it had taken place. When the family tried to reclaim her body, they were informed that she had already been buried. In other

125

cases prisoners have been executed after having been sentenced initially to a term of imprisonment, without any indication of additional legal proceedings having been brought against them.

After the Revolution

Immediately after the Revolution those executed were for the most part supporters of the Shah, although executions for sexual and drug offenses and common crimes also took place. During 1980 and the first half of 1981 executions were reported for alleged plots against the government, drug-smuggling and selling, espionage, collaboration with the Iraqi forces, sexual offenses, support of the Kurdish Democratic Party, murder and robbery. Baha'is and Jews were executed, usually on charges of espionage apparently based on the connections members of these religions have with Israel (Baha'i world headquarters are in Israel). Since the revolution more than 100 Baha'is have been executed. Amnesty International knows of no evidence to support the charge of espionage. Executions for all these offenses have continued, but during the second half of 1981 and 1982 most of those executed were members of organizations actively opposed to the authorities, most of whom had also been in opposition at the time of the Shah and had been among the most fervent supporters of the revolution.

Following the political disturbances which occurred after the departure of President Bani-Sadr, hundreds of executions took place within a very short time. Of the 2,616 executions known to Amnesty International which took place in 1981, 2,444 happened after 20 June. From the reports Amnesty International received at the time and subsequently it seems very likely that many of these executions took place without a trial, or at best after a summary trial. The sharp increase in executions from June 1981 was accompanied by growing conflict between supporters of the ruling Islamic Republican Party and its opponents.

Executing Children

There have been many reports of the execution of children and pregnant women. The People's Mujahideen Organization of Iran (PMOI), in their book *At War With Humanity . . .,*

The West German Section of AI created this poster. Text reads: thousands
of victims are the accusers—stop the executions.

published in May 1982, give the names of 12 pregnant women they say have been executed. In the same publication they give the names of 42 people of under 18 years of age who have been executed since 20 June 1981 and for some of these people show copies of birth certificates. Other examples of people under 18 who have been executed have been provided by Iranians from other political groups, interviewed by Amnesty International. Amir Molki, 16 years old, was reportedly arrested on 20 June at the Mujahideen demonstration and held in Evin Prison for three months before being executed without trial on 16 September 1981. In another account Amnesty International was told of the execution of a boy born in 1970 who had been taken to Evin Prison in June 1981 as a hostage for his father, who was in hiding. According to the account given to Amnesty International the boy had been rude to Ayatollah Gilani, the religious judge at Evin Prison. On 24 June 1981 Ayatollah Gilani was quoted in the *Guardian* newspaper as denying that children aged 13 and 14 were among those executed and saying, "None was less than 17. But anyhow, on the basis of Islam, a nine-year-old girl is considered mature. So there is no difference for us between a nine-year-old girl and a 40-year-old man, and it does not prohibit us from issuing any kind of sentence." On 20 September Assadollah Lajevardi, the Tehran Prosecutor General, reportedly said: "Even if a 12-year-old is found participating in an armed demonstration, he will be shot. The age doesn't matter." (*Times,* 21 September 1981). On 7 December the Head of Iran's Supreme Court, Ayatollah Mossavi Ardibili, told a press conference that death sentences were not passed on people under 18, although Islamic law said that people could be sentenced to death from the age of 16 (*Reuter,* 7 December 1981).

Amnesty International's cumulative total, based on published reports, for people executed since the revolution was 4,568 on 31 August 1982, but this must be regarded as a minimum figure, because increasingly executions have not been announced.

INTERPRETING EDITORIAL CARTOONS

This activity may be used as an individualized study guide for students in libraries and resource centers or as a discussion catalyst in small group and classroom discussions.

Although cartoons are usually humorous, the main intent of most political cartoonists is not to entertain. Cartoons express serious social comment about important issues. Using graphic and visual arts, the cartoonist expresses opinions and attitudes. By employing an entertaining and often light-hearted visual format, cartoonists may have as much or more impact on national and world issues as editorial or syndicated columnists.

Points to Consider

1. Examine the cartoon in this activity.

2. How would you describe the message in the cartoon? Try to describe the message in one to three sentences.

3. Do you agree with the message expressed in this cartoon? Why or why not?

4. Does the cartoon support the author's point of view in any of the readings in this publication? If the answer is yes, be specific about which reading or readings and why.

BIBLIOGRAPHY

BOOKS

Bedau, Hugo Adam. *The Death Penalty in America,* 3rd ed. (New York: Oxford Univ. Press, 1982).

Black, Charles L., Jr. *Capital Punishment: The Inevitability of Caprice and Mistake,* 2nd ed. (New York: W. W. Norton & Co., 1982).

Dike, Sarah T. *Capital Punishment in the United States: A Reconsideration of the Evidence* (Hackensack, N.J.: National Council on Crime and Delinquency, 1982).

Joyce, James Avery. *Capital Punishment* (New York: Thomas Nelson and Sons, 1961).

Lawrence, John. *The History of Capital Punishment* (New York: The Citadel Press, 1960).

Mackey, Philip E., ed. *Voices Against Death: American Opposition to Capital Punishment, 1787-1975* (New York: Franklin, 1976).

Magee, Doug. *Slow Coming Dark* (New York: The Pilgrim Press, 1980).

Meltsner, Michael. *Cruel and Unusual: The Supreme Court and Capital Punishment* (New York: Random House, 1973).

National Research Council. Panel on Research on Deterrent and Incapacitative Effects. Deterence and Incapacitation: Estimating the Effects of Criminal Sanctions on Crime Rates. (Washington: National Academy of Sciences, 1978) 431 pages.

Newman, Graeme. *Just and Painful* (London: Collier Macmillan, 1983).

Prettyman, Barrett, Jr. *Death and the Supreme Court* (New York: Harcourt, Brace, 1961).

Royal Commission on Capital Punishment, 1949-1953. *Report* (London: Her Majesty's Stationery Office, 1953).

Van den Haag, Ernest. *Punishing Criminals: Concerning a Very Old and Painful Question* (New York: Basic Books, 1975).

Van den Haag, Ernest and John P. Conrad. *The Death Penalty* (New York: Plenum Press, 1983).

MAGAZINES AND NEWSPAPERS

Anderson, G. M. "The Death Penalty in the United States, the Present Situation." *America* (Nov. 20, 1982) pp. 306-309.

Andersen, Kurt. "A 'More Palatable' Way of Killing." *Time* (Dec. 20, 1982) pp. 28-29.

Andersen, Kurt. "An Eye for an Eye." *Time* (Jan. 24, 1983) pp. 28-32, 35-36.

Bailey, William C. "Capital Punishment and Lethal Assaults Against Police." *Criminology* (Feb. 1982) pp. 608-25.

Berns, Walter. "Defending the Death Penalty." *Crime and Delinquency* (Oct. 1980) pp. 503-11.

Bowers, William J. and Glenn L. Pierce. "Arbitrariness and Discrimination Under Post-Furman Capital Statutes." *Crime and Delinquency* (Oct. 1980) pp. 563-635.

Breeck, D. "Decisions of Death." *The New Republic* (Dec. 12, 1983) pp. 18-21.

Cedarblom, J.B. and Gonzalo Munevar. "The Death Penalty: The Relevance of Deterrence." *Criminal Justice Review* (Spring, 1982) pp. 63-66.

Cohn, Haim H. "The Penology of the Talmud." *Israel Law Reviews* (1970) pp. 53-74.

Curran, William J. and Ward Casscells. "The Ethics of Medical Participation in Capital Punishment by Intravenous Drug Injection." *New England Journal of Medicine — 302* (1980) pp. 226-30.

Ehrlich, Isaac. "The Deterrent Effect of Capital Punishment: A Question of Life and Death." *American Economic Review — 65* (1975) pp. 397-417.

Espy, M. Watt, Jr. "Capital Punishment and Deterrence: What the Statistics Cannot Show." *Crime and Delinquency* (Oct., 1980) pp. 537-44.

Gest, T. "Death Penalty Again Haunts Supreme Court." *U.S. News and World Report* (Nov. 24, 1983) p. 54.

Gest, Ted. "The Noose Gets Tighter on Death Row." *U.S. News and World Report* (July 18, 1983) p. 21.

Greenberg, Jack. "Capital Punishment as a System." *Yale Law Journal* (April, 1982) pp. 908-36.

Hoekema, D.A. "Another Execution." *The Christian Century* (Sept. 8, 1982) p. 877.

Hoekema, D.A. "Capital Punishment: The Question of Justification." *The Christian Century* (March 28, 1979) pp. 338-42.

Jacoby, Joseph E. and Raymond Paternoster. "Sentencing Disparity and Jury Packing: Further Challenges to the Death Penalty." *Journal of Criminal Law & Criminology* (Spring, 1982) pp. 379-87.

Lempert, Richard O. "Desert and Deterrence: An Assessment of the Moral Bases of the Case for Capital Punishment." *Michigan Law Review* (May, 1981) pp. 1177-1231.

McCombs, Phil. "Capital Punishment Dilemma." *Washington Post* (June 13, 1982) pp. A1, A16-17 (June 14, 1982) pp. A1, A10 (June 15, 1982) p. A12.

Neapolitan, Jerry. "Support For and Opposition To Capital Punishment: Some Associated Social-Psychological Factors." *Criminal Justice and Behavior* (June, 1983) pp. 195-208.

Schwarzschild, Henry. "Any Man's Death." *Nation* (Oct. 27, 1979) pp. 388-89.

Spence, K. "Crime and Punishment." *National Review* (Sept. 16, 1983) p. 1140.

Stolz, Barbara Ann. "Congress and Capital Punishment: An Exercise in Symbolic Politics." *Law & Policy Quarterly* (April, 1983) pp. 157-80.

Walker, D.B. "The Death Penalty: Legal Cruelty?" *USA Today* (Nov., 1983) p. 70.

Wolfgang, Marvin E. and Marc Riedel. "Race, Judicial Discretion, and the Death Penalty." *Annals of the American Academy of Political and Social Science* 407 (1973) pp. 119-33.

Yunker, James A. "Testing the Deterrent Effect of Capital Punishment." *Criminology* (Feb., 1982) pp. 626-49.

"Do Judges Make Death Penalty an Empty Threat?" *U.S. News & World Report* (May 11, 1981) p. 72.

"High Court Upsets Death Penalty for Boy, 16, in Slaying of Trooper." *New York Times* (Jan. 20, 1982) p. A18.

"Revive the Death Penalty?" *U.S. News and World Report* (April 20, 1981) pp. 49-50.

"The Death Penalty." *Black Enterprise* (May, 1983) pp. 52-56.

"The Death Penalty in the United States." *America* (Nov. 20, 1982) pp. 306-12.

Government and Other Publications

Gallup, George. "Support for Death Penalty Greatest in 28 Years." Gallup Poll (Mar. 1, 1981) pp. 1-5.

Miller, Alan V., Capital Punishment as a Deterrent: A Bibliography. (Monticello, Ill.: Vance Bibliographies, 1980) 10 pages. Public Administration Series: Bibliography p-452.

Capital Punishment 1982, July 1983. Washington, Bureau of Justice Statistics; available from National Criminal Justice Reference Service, Rockville, MD., 1983. 4 p. (Bulletin, July 1983, NCJ-89395).

"Capital Punishment." Senate Committee on the Judiciary, 97th Congress, 1st Session, on S.114 (Washington: Government Printing Office, April-May, 1981)

"Sentencing in Capital Cases." Senate Committee on the Judiciary, Subcommittee on Criminal Justice, 95th Congress, 2nd Session, on H.R.13360. (Washington: Government Printing Office, 1978.

"To Establish Constitutional Procedures for the Imposition of Capital Punishment." Senate Subcommittee on Criminal Laws and Procedures, Committee on the Judiciary, 95th Congress, 1st Session, on S.1382. (Washington: Government Printing Office, May, 1977).

U.S. Department of Justice, Bureau of Justice Statistics. *Capital Punishment* (Washington: Government Printing Office). An annual publication.

"Execution by Injection." New York, WNET/Thirteen, 1982. 7 pages. The MacNeil/Lehrer Report (Dec. 9, 1982).

"The Court and the Death Penalty." New York, WNET/Thirteen, 1983. 7 pages. The MacNeil/Lehrer Report (July 6, 1983).